Julie Clinton is a gift—a godly woman filled with great strength, courage, grace, and beauty. *Bounce Back* will inspire and encourage you to walk more fully into your gifts and all God has called you to be.

—Margaret Feinberg, author of *Wonderstruck*

I have known Julie Clinton for over a decade and been involved with Extraordinary Women for almost as long. I have seen, firsthand, multiplied women learn to breathe, believe, and bounce back. In turn, that inspiration has helped me do the same in my own personal journey. I believe *Bounce Back* will have that same life-changing impact on you.

—Lisa Whelchel, actress, author, speaker

This world is not our home—and we sure see evidence of that every day, don't we? Yet we have a choice how we respond to it. Julie's excellent message shows us we don't have to live weighed down by disillusionment, disappointment, and depression—and that there are practical things we can do to bounce back! I *love* this advice, and every one of us needs to hear it!

—Shaunti Feldhahn, social researcher and
best-selling author of *For Women Only*

If you have experienced disappointment, failure, loss, or heartache, read this book! In *Bounce Back*, Julie Clinton shares practical, biblical principles that will help you to make the next right choices, get back up, and move in a positive direction. This book is filled with captivating stories and how-to action steps that will change your life for the better. Excellent for personal or small group study!

—Carol Kent, speaker and author, *Unquenchable*

Julie Clinton feels the heartbeat of women. From the Extraordinary Women conferences to your home, this book will compassionately lead you to a place of healing, encouragement, and rest. No matter where we are in this journey of life, Julie reminds us, we can all bounce back from difficulty with God's help.

—Linda Mintle, PhD, best-selling author, radio host, national blogger, speaker, and vice president of PureMedia Group, Inc.

I've had the privilege of traveling with Julie all across the US, ministering with the Extraordinary Women conferences. In every city, I have watched God provide hope and courage for the broken. *Bounce Back* tells the stories of women like you and me, women who dare to believe that God is bigger than their pain. Women who are learning to trust a God who delights in redeeming and rescuing His daughters. If you need a fresh start, Bounce Back is the book for you!

—Angela Thomas, best-selling author and speaker

Every day we need to be reminded that we serve a God who is in the business of restoring and redeeming the broken, hurting, and doubting places of our heart. This book serves as that breathtaking reminder. Julie's writing is honest, inspiring, and life-giving to any woman who may be questioning her worth and purpose in life; which, let's face it, is all of us at some point, perhaps many points, along our journey. This offering is a beautiful gift to the hearts of women throughout all generations.

—Kasey Van Norman, best-selling author, Bible teacher, and child rescue advocate

Every woman needs to know she is not alone in her struggles and heartbreak and that she can start over again. Julie Clinton—whom I have known, worked with, and respected for decades—has a heart of compassion for the deep needs and longings of women. In her book *Bounce Back*, she encourages us to understand that no matter what we have gone through, we can face life with a renewed sense of purpose and hope. Women everywhere should have this book!

—Stormie Omartian, best-selling author of The Power of a Praying series (28 million books sold worldwide) including *The Power of a Praying Wife, The Power of a Praying Woman*, and *Prayer Warrior*

Julie Clinton's heart beats hard after Christ's, beats in gentle rhythm with Christ's. I am profoundly moved by Christ in her as she powerfully draws on our stories, the stories of women, to draw each of us closer to Him—to find a reviving, fresh hope in Him.

—Ann Voskamp, *New York Times* best-selling author of *One Thousand Gifts: A Dare to Live Fully Right Where You Are*

What a wonderful resource for all of us who have experienced loss or times of loneliness. Julie's practical advice combined with many women's stories help us find answers to the nagging questions that often seem too big or too deep to ask a friend. Thank you, Julie, for bringing this much-needed wisdom to the table.

—Lysa TerKeurst, *New York Times* best-selling author and president of Proverbs 31 Ministries

I love a book that offers practical steps, biblical truths, real-life examples, and the wisdom that can only be gained from experience. Julie Clinton has poured her heart into these pages, teaching us how to breathe, believe, and truly bounce back. If you're discouraged or your faith is flagging, here are the hope-filled answers you're looking for!

—Liz Curtis Higgs, best-selling author of *Bad Girls of the Bible*

After walking with Julie as a friend and being a part of the EW team for several years I can tell you, this book is an honest reflection of her heart and the essence of the EW conference experience. Addressing people where they really live with honesty and empathy. Keeping it real but giving practical principles that can help put back together the pieces of a shattered heart and a dismantled life. This is a must read for yourself as well as friends who need an encouraging word and a clear-cut path to bouncing back after being deflated by disappointments or setbacks.

—Michelle McKinney Hammond,
best-selling author, singer, and television cohost

If your heart is empty, or your dreams are lost . . . here's the hope you need! Drawing from stories of women just like you and me, my friend Julie Clinton shares powerful principles to help us all find new hope and a fresh start in life. No matter what your circumstances, God has not forgotten you. He longs to heal and restore you from the inside out. So grab some friends, dive in, and discover how you can bounce back!

—Jennifer Rothschild, author,
Lessons I Learned in the Dark and *Self Talk, Soul Talk*
Founder, womensministry.net and Fresh Grounded Faith Events

Are you tired? Worn out? Desperate for change? Whether it's a divorce, cancer, a job loss, or a wayward child, the weight of grief and disappointment can be crushing. In *Bounce Back*, Julie Clinton reminds us of God's unchanging promises and offers a clear plan to help women regain their purpose, joy, and passion for life.

—Elisa Morgan, speaker, author of *The Beauty of Broken*, publisher of
FullFill, President Emerita, MOPS International

Having just walked through a hard season of trial, I can tell you that the words in this book breathe life into a weary soul. No matter your trial, Julie's words turn us away from keeping a list of what's wrong with our life and writing a list of possibilities. It's time to *Bounce Back*.

—Dannah Gresh, best-selling author and founder, Secret Keeper Girl

Simply put, I love Julie Clinton's heart and passion for women to find hope, healing, and life in Christ. *Bounce Back* is a vibrant example of her heart!

—Donna VanLiere, *New York Times* best-selling author of
The Good Dream and *The Christmas Shoes*

WHEN YOUR HEART IS EMPTY
AND YOUR DREAMS ARE LOST

*B*OUNCE
BACK

JULIE
CLINTON

WORTHY®
PUBLISHING

Library of Congress Control Number: 2013956965

For foreign and subsidiary rights, contact rights@worthypublishing.com

Cover Design: Susan Browne Design
Cover Illustration: Getty Images
Interior Design and Typesetting: Christopher D. Hudson & Associates, Inc

To the EW team—who travel and give selflessly so that women all across America can find new courage and fresh faith to bounce back! Thank you for your faithful ministry!

Contents

Acknowledgments

This project would not have been possible without the support, prayer, encouragement, and feedback of my family, friends, and professional colleagues. My sincerest thanks . . . and hats off to each of you!

I want to acknowledge Jan Dargatz for her amazing ability and talent to help me craft this work. Words fall short to communicate my deep appreciation for you, Jan! Along with that, a special note of appreciation goes out to Tom Winters and especially Ted Squires for believing in me and standing behind the vision of *Bounce Back*.

I am eternally grateful to the incredible publishing team at Worthy—including Byron Williamson and Jeana Ledbetter—for their belief in the EW message and for giving me this platform to influence and encourage women from every walk of life. I also want to thank Laura Captari for her input and editing to help bring this project home.

To the EW team—you are the hands and feet of Jesus. Thank you for dedicating long hours during the week and on the weekends to faithfully serve Christ and women across the nation. I am grateful and feel extremely blessed to serve with you.

To all who have attended the EW conferences over the years and shared your stories—your courage to make tough decisions and take action to change your lives inspires me. You are a testament to the healing power of God, who longs for each of His daughters to bounce back!

I also want to acknowledge my mother, who daily shows me how to fight for joy and live fully. I appreciate every moment we share together, Mom, and have learned so much from you!

As always, I don't know what I'd do without my husband, Tim, and my children, Megan and Zach. You guys make the world a beautiful place for me. I love you so much!

And to my Lord and Savior—Your never-ending love and faithfulness carry me each day. May You get all the glory and use this book to bring renewed hope to all of us who feel like our hearts are empty, and our dreams are lost. You are our Redeemer—and there is nothing too hard for You!

Foreword

by Karen Kingsbury

The year was 1997 and I'd just given birth to our third child—a son named Austin. From the beginning Austin looked like an athlete—a football player type like his daddy. But there was a problem. Austin wasn't breathing right. Instead of the usual even-paced breaths, Austin's came more in fits and starts. "He's a fast breather," the doctor told us. "Nothing to worry about."

But I did worry. After three weeks of fast breathing, Austin began gasping for air. His little chest would rise and fall with each breath, and his fingernails were turning blue. My instincts told me the doctor had missed something. I took Austin back in that Monday, and as he listened to Austin's heartbeat, the doctor's expression changed. Immediately he ordered an EKG, and once he saw those results he told us the grim news.

"Your baby has a serious heart defect. You need to take him to Children's Hospital right away."

Just like that we were over our heads in waves of a crisis we never saw coming. The details were a blur—then and now—but I remember getting a call from my sister, Trish. At the time we lived in Portland, Oregon, and Trish lived in California. "He can't have heart surgery," she said, "We haven't even met him yet."

Somehow my words were calm. "Trust Jesus. You'll meet Austin one day—here or in heaven."

That night in the neonatal intensive care unit of Doern-becher Children's Hospital, we gave Austin a bath. I ran my fingers over his perfect back—the place where the next morning a surgeon would cut through and use a rib spreader to replace Austin's aorta with the artery from his left arm. *Please, God, show me how to come back from this*, I prayed. *I trust You. I do. But please let this count for something.*

The chances were against Austin surviving the surgery, but the next day after a long six hours in the waiting room, we received the news we had prayed for. Austin had survived. The doctor thought he would be fine. "He may always be small and sickly," he warned us. "But I believe he'll make it through."

We thanked God and began a six-week period in and out of intensive care. We accepted the fact that our little boy would always be little—sickly even—and after he came home for good, we prayed about what was next. We had planned to have other children, but the doctor warned us that future kids would have the same problem Austin had or worse. So we decided we were finished having biological children.

But we still had room in our hearts and home for more children. A year later the answer became clear. We would adopt two little boys from Haiti. Then came the next surprise. I went to pick up the boys in April 2001 and they were a trio of best friends. Inseparable. I called my husband. "Honey," I told him, "there aren't two but three boys."

Donald simply smiled through the phone lines. "Two, three. That's fine."

And so our family doubled overnight.

Today I think about that terrible time, learning of Austin's heart defect and his life-threatening surgery, and then knowing we couldn't have more children. God showed us how to move on in the middle of the most difficult time in our lives. Not only that, but He blessed us with three more sons because of Austin's condition.

I especially find myself thinking about it when I'm at Austin's football games. I watch my six-foot-five son running for a touchdown, and I smile at the doctor's warning about him being small and sickly. God didn't only use that time in our lives to teach me to trust Him. He used it to teach me something else.

How to bounce back.

An Ongoing Opportunity to Heal and to Grow

This book can be read as a source of personal inspiration. It can also be used for study—either personally or in small groups. Let me call your attention to the reflection guide following the last chapter; this final section gives additional material for you to consider alone or to discuss with others. You'll find Bible passages that dovetail with the content in each of the seven chapters.

I strongly encourage you to consider a small-group study with members in your church fellowship. Decide together how you might use this book to reach out to others who do not know Jesus as their Savior. You certainly can take more than one study session to deal with each chapter. I know one group that did an eight-chapter study over a twenty-week time period. As one member of that group said, "We took our time and God honored the time we took."

Always be on the alert for application. Ask the Lord often, "How can I put this information to use in my life, not only to help myself, but to help another person?" I believe that is a question God always delights in answering!

Remember always that the Lord desires to heal you and make you whole—in every area of your life. He desires to use you as a vessel for pouring out His love and mercy to others.

No woman is ever too broken to be of value to the Lord. No woman is ever beyond God's ability to fill her empty heart and to make her a blessing.

I believe in God's ability to help you *Bounce Back!*

Your sister in Christ now and forever,

Julie

Face the Trouble Behind the Smile

After you have suffered a little while, the God of all grace,
who has called you to his eternal glory in Christ, will
himself restore, confirm, strengthen, and establish you.
—*1 Peter 5:10 (ESV)*

In the middle of difficulty lies opportunity.
—*Albert Einstein*

I look into the beautiful, shining faces of literally thousands of women every year. I can close my eyes right now and see so many of these women with sharp clarity—in many cases, I can recall the sound of their voices.

The vast majority of them have a desire to be women of faith, with spiritual depth and vibrancy.

They are mature and accomplished women who, in many cases, have families and careers.

They are seeking women, wanting deeper, richer, and more meaningful lives.

Even so . . .

Just behind their smiles and warm greetings . . .

I often see a depth of pain and longing that is immense and persistent. In their eyes I see hurt. Anger. Sadness. Discouragement. Hopelessness. Desperation. I count it a high privilege to be able to pray with many of them, and to give at least a few words of encouragement.

There was Susan, who started her first sentence to me with a smile that dissolved into tears and that ended in a long, silent hug. When we were finally able to converse a bit, she shared with me that her husband of twenty-eight years had walked away earlier in the year to be with a woman half his age—a waitress he had met at a café, with whom he'd had a one-night fling that turned into an affair. She wasn't sure if he'd be back or if she'd want him if he did come back. She was conflicted and angry and didn't want to have either set of emotions.

There was Audra, who had lost her mother to a suffering disease and ultimately dementia. She couldn't stop asking, "Why didn't God step in and heal her? Why didn't God allow her to stay mentally and emotionally strong?" Audra believed her mother was now safely with the Lord in paradise, but she was still reeling from two years of intense caregiving and the deep pain of loss. Her mother had been her best friend.

There was Cynthia, who had started having nightmares related to intense sexual abuse from an uncle when she was a child. "Why now?" she questioned. She admitted that at times she felt as if she was losing her mind. She had not thought about these experiences for more than two decades, but now she felt haunted by them. She dreaded going to bed at night, fearful of the nightmares that seemed to be recurring more regularly.

There was Dorothy, an older woman who said she desperately wanted to be free of the resentment she had held against her former husband for more than thirty years. He had put her and their children through bankruptcy and the loss of a comfortable lifestyle and then abandoned the family, leaving her to fend for herself financially and raise three young children as a single mother. And then, like bad icing on a bad cake, he had reappeared with a new wife and two adult children, asking for her forgiveness "twenty-five years too late." She said, "I told him I forgave him, but I really didn't. I felt angry and cornered by his asking for forgiveness in the presence of these three people I didn't know. That was several years ago. Rather than feel better as time goes by, I feel even deeper resentment. I don't want to be a bitter old woman."

There was Maryanne, who had lost a fifth pregnancy, this latest one at six months. She had a deep and abiding desire for a baby. The miscarriages were wearing on her relationship with her husband, especially as they explored expensive options for medical intervention to assist them to conceive or, in her words, "to heal my broken uterus." She was not at all interested in pursuing adoption, and she certainly was not interested in even considering a fulfilling life without a "child of our own." She was almost frantic in her quest for a baby and had a suspicion that God might not be as good as she had been told He was.

Each of these women had a deep desire for:

- *God's presence.* They each wanted to feel God in their lives, emotionally and spiritually. They wanted a deeper, dearer, more direct relationship with a loving Lord.
- *a personal miracle.* They wanted new freedom and healing of a kind they knew could only come from Christ Jesus.
- *the ability to let go of the past.* They each wanted a release from emotions they knew were negative and limiting, but they had no clue about how to release their pain.
- *more enthusiasm for living.* They each had a deep longing for more energy and more zest in their lives. As one woman said, "I want to get up in the morning eager for the new day. I'm tired of feeling that the best place for me to live is in bed with the covers pulled up over my head."
- *greater authenticity and fulfillment.* They each felt a need to be "the real me" without criticism or limitation. They wanted fulfillment in their life and ministry, including a strong sense of purpose and a role to play in God's plan for the world.

These women are not isolated examples. They are the mainstream of our world and of the church. Half of the women who come to our conferences are single, for various reasons. Some of them are married, yet still *feel* single because their husbands are inattentive, absent, or unsympathetic to them most of the time. A significant percentage of them have suffered or are suffering from a stress-related disorder or an eating disorder.

Most of them have endured pain or disappointment of some variety—in their relationships, in their health, in their work life, in their childhoods. The pain has lingered and festered and they long to be free of it. They have a deep desire to break out of the "what if," "if only," and "paralyzed in the present" state in which they find themselves.

They often feel overwhelmed, stressed out to the max, and stuck in their lives.

When I ask the women to describe their lives today, I often hear these words:

- overstressed
- overworked
- underappreciated
- underpaid
- burnt out

Many of the women admit to having more than one of these words as a descriptor for their lives—and some lay claim to all five!

I can guarantee you this: the women who provide these descriptive words do not want to live the way they are living. Most of them simply don't know how to break out of being burdened, in bondage, or carrying emotional baggage that is too heavy for one person to carry. They realize something is broken, but they don't know how to fix it.

They want to be set free, break out, and bounce back!

They are the reason for this book.

You may not directly relate to Susan, Audra, Cynthia, Dorothy, or Maryanne, described above. But I suspect you do relate to their feelings and their yearnings. And if not you personally, you very likely know someone who does have their experiences, feelings, or deep longings.

My overarching word to you today is this: *hope*.

God does love you.

He does want a better life for you.

And He does have a way for you to move from where you are, to the better life of your future. You can bounce back.

CHAPTER 1

Decide to Breathe, Believe, and Bounce Back

Everyone has a fair turn to be as great as he pleases.
—Jeremy Collier

"My life is out of control."

I knew from the way she spoke these words, punctuated by her hands held up as if they might never hold anything or anybody again, that she was seriously serious.

"What's wrong?" I asked.

"Everything!" She went on to give me a potent list of problems, including:

"My husband divorced me."

"He has taken up with a slut he met in a bar. I didn't even know he went to bars."

"He got half the house and most of our money, and there's not enough for me to buy out the other half of the house or pay my monthly bills."

"He has turned the kids against me."

"He wants to have me committed for mental evaluation. *He's* the one with the mental problems."

"He wants nothing to do with God or the church or my family or *our* family."

When she paused to inhale, I said, "Let me give you this one lifeline: you *can* do something, and here is what it is: you can make a decision *right now* about how you are going to respond to all of this. You—yes, you—*can* make a choice with your will about what you are going to do in the next few minutes, the next hour, the rest of today."

She grew quiet and fixed her eyes on mine.

"But . . . " she started.

I interjected. "I want you to repeat after me these three words: *I can decide*."

She did.

And then she asked, "But what can I decide? What decisions can *I* make?"

"There are three main decisions that are totally in your power and under your control." I say this to you as well.

You Are in Charge of Three Main Decisions

There are three main decisions that are totally within your ability to make and then act on.

The Decision to *Breathe*

We all breathe, of course. We *must* breathe to live. Scientists tell us we can't continue to exist if we are denied oxygen for more than three to four minutes.

The kind of breathing I'm talking about is not physical. It is emotional, spiritual—it is a breathing of the *soul*.

Just as He created us to breathe physically, God calls us to breathe on the inside of our being—emotionally and spiritually.

**God calls us to breathe on the inside of our being—
emotionally and spiritually.**

There are two main principles to consider here:

First, you *must exhale* before you *can inhale*. Many of us are holding on to negative emotions, reliving negative encounters or negative experiences over and over and over again. We need to let go of them before we can fully embrace new and positive experiences and relationships.

Second, *you must have a distinct separation between "letting go" and "taking on."* The apostle Paul wrote several passages in the New Testament about this. He told the early Christians there were certain behaviors and attitudes they needed to "put off" so they could "put on" a more Christlike identity (for example, see Ephesians 4:21–24).

We all know about layering when it comes to clothing. Heidi, who wore all the clothes she owned on a trek up a mountain to visit her grandfather, is perhaps the ultimate example of someone layering her wardrobe! Wardrobe layering has one great advantage, which can also be regarded as its major disadvantage: layering causes greater warmth. Dressing in layers is great for a ski trip in the winter. It is terrible for going to the beach (unless you're trying to hide something!).

Layering also adds bulk, even if you're layering very skinny fabrics. Not all layers of clothing are compatible—one type of fabric can cause another type of fabric to bunch or ride up. The result is discomfort!

In emotional terms, layering often occurs when we rehearse a problem or the pain associated with it to the point that we are adding multiple remembrances of the experience to our memory bank. The end result is very often increasing anger (heat) toward a person or group and, along with it, increased bitterness or resentment. The ongoing result is one of inner discomfort—we generally don't *like* to feel angry, bitter, or resentful. But once those feelings take root in us, we must confront them directly and deal with them forcefully.

The process usually involves a degree of separation— a stepping back or a slight distancing—so we can gain new perspective and have greater clarity about what we are doing and what we must do to be free of all those layers.

We need to shed the old hurt so we are *ready* to take on a new joy.

The truth is we do need to take off an old garment before we can put on a new garment if we want the new garment to fit sleekly and be comfortable. The same is true for our emotions.

We need to shed the old hurt so we are *ready* to take on a new joy.

I learned many years ago that most animals wounded in the wild seek immediately to go to their lair or den to nurse their wounds and rest. They allow a wound to heal, and that takes a little time. Animals intuitively know that sleep is their best medicine, and sleeping in a safe place is not only therapeutic but welcome.

I'm certainly not advocating that a woman who is wounded take to her bed! That's what some women do to escape the emotional struggles of life, and while it may be helpful for a couple of days, it is *never* truly therapeutic to withdraw to your bedroom with the shades drawn. If you are sleeping in order to get well from an injury, disease, or trauma, that's one thing. If you are sleeping in order to escape your own reality and future, that's another!

What I am advocating is that you find a place to which you might withdraw for a short period of time in order to gain perspective. This might be a personal retreat or time with friends. It might be a visit to a spa. It might be a few days at a local retreat center or going to a women's conference.

Not long ago I met a woman named Jeanne who told me she periodically goes to a nearby convent for several quiet days of prayer and Bible reading. Jeanne is not of the same religious affiliation as the women who run the convent, but she said, "I am welcomed there as a Christian seeking more of Christ. And that truly is the case. I've gone to the convent to hear from the Lord, to study the Scriptures about a situation I'm facing, or to search my own heart for areas in which I might be harboring an unforgiving or distrustful attitude."

"What kinds of situations have compelled you to go to this place?" I asked.

"One time I went because I knew I needed to make some adjustments in my marriage. I had been blaming my husband for our problems but I secretly knew that I was contributing to them in some way. I went to hear from the Lord about *me*, not him.

"Another time I went because I felt as if I had hit a brick wall in my job. Everything I was doing seemed to be criticized strongly by people who had for years been giving me affirmation and approval. I needed to distance myself from work and take a new look at what I was doing and why.

"And yet another time I went because I just felt *dry*. I had heard people talk about wilderness periods in their faith walk and suddenly I knew what they meant. I felt as if my prayers were bouncing off the ceiling and that God was very far away."

"Were you totally alone on these spiritual retreats?"

"Yes," she said. "I went to the chapel once a day in the morning, and I had a simple, quiet breakfast, lunch, and evening tea with the women who lived there. But they didn't intrude on my solitude. I knew they were there if I wanted or needed them, but they weren't hovering over me."

"What happened as a result of your time alone with the Lord?"

She laughed. "Well, I made some very dramatic changes

in the way I treated my husband, mostly in the way I prayed for him and began to praise God for him. When it came to my job, I sought a *new* job—and got one. It has been much more challenging and the new company is both stronger financially and operates in a more professional manner. As for the wilderness time in my faith journey—I walked through that. I learned a great deal about prayer and especially about the offering of thanksgiving and praise. I realized I was all about asking God for things I wanted rather than thanking and praising Him for His provision of all the things I truly needed."

What good results!

"If you could sum up these times in one or two words, what would you say?" I asked.

She replied, "I learned to *breathe*."

**Retreating for a time to breathe is not running
from life. Rather, it is running *to* the Lord!**

Retreating for a time to breathe is not running *from* life. Rather, it is running *to* the Lord! It is running to the One who truly can heal you and restore you inside and out. It is running to the One who takes on your burdens and exchanges them for a life that is truly "free." It is in Christ Jesus that we are to "live and move and have our being" (Acts 17:28).

When we exhale our problem to the Lord in confession and prayer, coupled with thanksgiving and praise, we find ourselves much more willing and able to inhale His life-giving Spirit, including an abundance of peace and joy.

The Decision to *Believe*

You are the only person who truly can decide with certainty what—and in Whom—you will believe. The good news is that nobody can rip these decisions from your mind and heart. What you believe with deep conviction and commitment becomes who you are. Your values and your beliefs are the foundation for all you will say and do in your life. They are ingrained in you in such a way that they *become* your instinctual responses.

The good news here is also this: if you have adopted a belief or value that you discover is *not* in line with God's Word, you can change your mind! You can decide to adopt a new belief.

Let me give you a few words of caution:

First, *beliefs are meant to be foundational and therefore must be taken very seriously*. We are not emotional or spiritual chameleons, changing our minds continually in order to blend in with whatever crowd of people in which we find ourselves. We must take our values and beliefs very seriously. They are at the core of good relationships and of all "good works" that honor God.

Second, *not all of us were taught the "right things" as children*. I have encountered numerous women who take great joy in what they learn at our women's conferences. A woman named Flo came to me one time and said, "I'm so excited! I have heard things this weekend that I suspected were true, but they were contrary to what my mother and grandmother had told me as a child. I realized this weekend that Mom and Grandmommy had probably been taught wrong by *their* mothers. They were passing on what they thought was good, but they were not passing on what God's Word says. Now that I know what my heavenly Father thinks and wants, I have a whole new frame of mind. And I feel free to explore more fully what I might do with my life and how I might serve the Lord."

As you consider what you have been taught as a belief or value, line it up against the Word of God. If what you believe doesn't line up with God's Word. . . go with the Word of God!

If what you believe doesn't line up with God's Word . . .
go with the Word of God!

I learned a good lesson about this from a woman named Cherie. She said, "Julie, my mother and father were people who never took any risks, and they didn't want me to take any risks either. They continually told me what I shouldn't undertake as new ventures or pursue as new goals, and they spelled out in vivid detail all the ways I was setting myself up for failure. When I continued to take risks with my dreams and goals, they adopted a slightly new tack—which is actually one they had started out with when I was just a little girl. They began to tell me that I wasn't smart enough, wasn't talented enough, or wasn't of the right social class to be a leader or innovator. And the sad thing is they almost convinced me they were right."

"What did you do to break out of that?" I asked.

"I decided that I would go to my Bible and learn what God had to say about me!"

"And?"

"And I learned that God says I am made in His image [Genesis 1:26]. God said He had made me to be the head, not the tail—to be at the top and never at the bottom [Deuteronomy 28:13]. I learned that God was my Creator and He had made me to multiply and have dominion and to take charge of things in order to help create a better world [Genesis 1:28–30]. I learned that I do have amazing talents and abilities that He built into me, and that I am to use those abilities to help others. The more I read God's Word and really *studied* it, the more my beliefs and values shifted toward what *God* said about me. The old tapes in my mind of my mother's and father's voices began to fade. God's Word became the strong voice."

How many women grow up with old tapes that are inaccurate! If you believe this is true for you, embark on your own discovery about what God says in His Word. He has plans and dreams for you that are glorious, and He has a one-of-a-kind job for you to fill on this earth. When you discover His ideas and His plans and begin to live them out, your believing will take on a whole new vibrancy.

Third, *beliefs should be continually reaffirmed*. Once we know the truth and are walking in the highest and best values and beliefs, we must continually remind ourselves of what we believe and in whom we believe. As my friend Angela said one day, "I may not have all the answers, but I know who *does* have all the answers. And I'm walking through life clinging to His hand!"

There are many ways to reaffirm your values and beliefs, but from my experience, these methods of reaffirmation nearly always take me back to the Word of God. I have heard of women who:

- daily recite the Lord's Prayer and use it as an outline to speak to their own hearts and minds about God providing for them, forgiving them, delivering them from evil, and ascending to the throne of their soul where He will have all power and authority and glory.

- frequently meditate on and at times even recite classic Christian works, such as the Nicene Creed or Apostles' Creed. These ancient statements have been recited routinely by Christians for nearly two thousand years and can really help anchor personal faith. They proclaim the nature of God the Father, God the Son, and God the Spirit. They allow a person to give voice to what she believes about her eternal salvation and about her future in the Lord.

- have developed a set of personal "verses to live by." These are verses they have committed to memory, and also ones they have written on small note cards that they carry with them. They have written verses that are especially meaningful to them as reminders of God's presence with them and about what God desires—and requires—of them as His faithful followers.

One of the most powerful ways of reaffirming your beliefs and values is this: choose to read a portion of God's Word every day. I recommend a selection of verses—some from the book of Proverbs, some from the Psalms, and some from the Gospels or other New Testament books. As you read, ask the Lord to speak to you through His Word. When you come across a verse that seems especially pertinent to what you are going through or what you are facing in your near future, stop and voice it aloud as a little prayer: "Lord, this is for *me*. Thank You for showing me this. Help me to remember it and live it out!"

You may want to underline that verse in your Bible or put a date next to it. You may want to write it out as your Bible truth for the day and stick it in your purse so you can look at it again during the day. You can definitely make it a prayer throughout the day: "Lord, You said . . . I believe. Let it come to pass!"

One of my favorite promises in all of Scripture is Isaiah 41:10:

So do not fear, for I am with you;
>do not be dismayed, for I am your God.
I will strengthen you and help you;
>I will uphold you with my righteous
>right hand.

On crazy days, I find myself whispering, "Lord, you said that you are always with me. You commanded me not to fear. God, you promised to strengthen and help me. To uphold me. I believe. Let it come to pass!"

A woman once commented to me, "All this sounds like brainwashing."

I readily agreed! Yes, I do believe we need to wash our brains. I wash my hands and face, brush my teeth, wash my hair, put my clothes in the laundry, wash the dishes. Why not wash my mind? In fact, the Bible tells me that Christ "gave himself up for [the church] to make her holy, cleansing her by the washing with water through the word" (Ephesians 5:25–26).

God has designed a one-of-a-kind way for you to bounce back.

I continued, "Bad brainwashing is when someone attempts to control your thinking to do what that person says. *Good* brainwashing is when you invite the Lord to instruct and guide your thinking. *Good* brainwashing is submitting your own brain to God's Word so the Lord might cleanse the thoughts of your heart through the inspiration of His Spirit."

I choose to be washed anew every day by the Word of God.

The Decision to *Bounce Back*

There are a million and more ways to bounce back. Bouncing back is highly individualized. The way in which the Lord leads you to bounce back is going to be *similar* to the bounce-back actions of others, but at the same time it is going to be unique to you. You are a one-of-a-kind creation of God, and God has designed a one-of-a-kind way for you to bounce back.

Keep in mind as you explore various ways to bounce back that the process of bouncing back is just that—a *process*. It occurs over time. Nobody ever bounces back from extreme negativity to profound positivity in a minute, an hour, or a day. You may experience a form of spiritual deliverance or emotional transformation in an instant—but the manifestation of that in the routines, habits, and choices of your life is an ongoing process that is intended by God to grow stronger and more profound day by day.

Bouncing back is:

- *active.* It is the bold taking of a new step, often moving in a new direction.
- *intentional.* It is something we choose to do with our will. We may receive wise counsel from others, but in the end, the way in which we bounce back is something that must be of our own volition.
- *behavioral.* Bouncing back involves things we speak and things we do—both are key aspects of behavior. In bouncing back, you will find the Lord leading you to say new things, or to say old things in a new way or with greater meaning. You will find the Lord leading you to try new things and to engage in new forms of ministry to others around you. You will find yourself experi-

encing new insights into God's Word, and along the way find that He is leading you to new applications of His Word in your daily life and dearest relationships.

The process of following the Lord is never stagnant. It is neither dull nor boring. It is always challenging—but challenging in a way that always points toward the use of your faith. The bounce-back process proclaims, "I *can* . . . with God's help!"

Bouncing back is *not* like bouncing on a trampoline—which can be great fun but goes nowhere. Those who routinely bounce on a trampoline for fun seem to love the challenge of jumping higher and higher, even to the point they can do spins and twists and somersaults. But for a jump to be successful, the person jumping needs to come down in the same place. There's good exercise involved, but not real purpose or progress.

Bouncing back emotionally and spiritually is all about purpose and progress. Three steps forward and two steps back is progress. Be realistic.

**Bouncing back emotionally and spiritually
is all about purpose and progress.**

God's desire is always that we move onward, forward, and higher!

- *Onward.* We leave the past behind us and press on toward greater purpose. We do not necessarily leave the people and circumstances of our life behind. In truth, we are wise to *not* leave behind our most valued relationships, our church family, or those good relationships that are mutually interdependent and joyful. We *are* wise, in contrast, to lay aside all sin and all weights of responsibility and commitments we have developed that are *not* beneficial to our receiving God's rewards and blessings. We must learn to take responsibility for only what we can control and leave the rest in God's hands.

- *Forward.* God always calls us forward. He has new mercies for us every day. He has a future that is ours to claim. There's more that lies ahead of us—and God has ways for us to achieve and experience things we haven't even *thought* to ask for or imagine (Ephesians 3:20).

- *Upward.* With the apostle Paul, we must "press on toward the goal to win the prize for which God has called [us] heavenward in Christ Jesus" (Philippians 3:14). The things to which God calls us are always things with heavenly purpose and an eternal reward. God desires that as we bounce back, we do so in a way that enhances our witness for Christ and encourages others to trust God and receive all that He has for them.

The Bible gives us these wonderful words of encouragement:

Let us throw off everything that hinders and the sin that so easily entangles. And let us run with perseverance the race marked out for us, fixing our eyes on Jesus, the pioneer and perfecter of faith. For the joy set before him he endured the cross, scorning its shame, and sat down at the right hand of the throne of God. Consider him who endured such opposition from sinners, so that you will not grow weary and lose heart. (Hebrews 12:1–3)

The Rhythm of Recovery

You not only *can* make decisions to breathe, believe, and bounce back . . . but *only* you can make these decisions. Nobody can make them for you.

You not only *must* make these decisions . . . but your ability to bounce back into a vibrancy of life won't happen until you do.

The ability to make decisions about how you will breathe, about what you choose to believe and hold as foundational values, and about how you will bounce back are directly related to an increasing level of spiritual maturity. These abilities are absolutely essential to growth in your relationship with the Lord and to developing good relationships with other people. These abilities are also essential to your own peace of mind, your personal level of joy, and the pursuit of your future dreams and goals.

The ability to decide is a critically important factor when it comes to getting off dead center and back into the flow of productive, meaningful life. Even small decisions, often made at the daily level, are important.

I once had a good conversation with a woman named Terri. She had been suffering from depression and was well on her way back to vibrancy. She said, "I finally realized that nobody was going to pick me up out of the pit in which I found myself. The counselors could help. The medications prescribed for me might help as well. But in the end, I had to make some very basic decisions. And they were oh so small in the beginning. One day, for example, I said right out loud, 'Terri, get yourself up and get dressed and put on some makeup and comb your hair and take the dog out for a long walk.' I did just that. And when I got home, I felt just a little better. Not much, but a little. Another day I said, 'Okay, girl, today is the day you must get this pile of clothes to the dry cleaners.' And I did. I felt a little better. And so it went. A decision to 'get well' or 'take on a new challenge' was just too big. But after a long series of small decisions, one day I *was* able to tell my counselor with new resolve, 'I think I've decided to get better—not just get back, but get *better*.'"

"And what did he say?" I asked.

He said, "All right! I've been waiting and believing for this day. Let's go for *better*!"

As you make choices to move onward, forward, and upward, always choose to go for *better*! The time you spend in the *breathing* stage may be short or long. It is a time that you determine according to your need.

As you make choices to move onward, forward, and upward, always choose to go for *better*!

The time you spend in *believing* is also subject to your need and desires. You may have lots of values and beliefs to sort out and redefine. Or you may find this a time of affirmation for the validity and applicability of your beliefs. Take the time you need to find solid substance and good reasons for what you consider to be the rock-solid foundation on which you stand and walk through life.

The experience of *bouncing back* is going to be lifelong. You will *always* be moving onward, forward, and upward until the moment you cross over life's finish line and enter paradise. Don't be discouraged by that. Simply choose to take the next best step.

An Ongoing Cycle for Strength and Growth

The three Bs—*breathe, believe,* and *bounce back*—generally occur in a cycle, which actually functions more like an upward *spiral*.

Life can be lived fully even in the midst of disappointments, discouraging events, and difficult problems. The old saying, "I never promised you a rose garden," is true in every area of life. God never promised His people a life of leisure, luxury, or total laughter. He has made it very clear to His people through the ages—in both His Word and in examples of people who were faithful to Him—that He is the Lord who is in control of *all* things and the One who helps us achieve balance in times that seem to pull us apart and chop us up.

No, God didn't promise us a waltz through a rose garden. But He *did* make these promises:

- "I will never leave you nor forsake you" (Joshua 1:5).
- "I will send you a Helper" (John 14:16, paraphrased).

- "I am a Rewarder of those who diligently seek Me" (Hebrews 11:6, paraphrased).

We are wise to cling to what God has promised, rather than to cling to what we wish God would do for us. God has an unending supply of provision and protection for us—on His terms and in His timing. He has promised us unlimited access to Himself and, therefore, to an unlimited amount of His presence.

As you *breathe* . . .

And *believe* . . .

And then prepare to *bounce back* . . .

Ask the Lord very directly and with faith to help you, guide you, and surround you with His love and peace. Open yourself to His presence.

Is it possible to breathe and believe at the same time? Yes. It may involve two different issues in your life. It is also possible to pause to breathe and believe about one problem or hurtful experience even as you move on to bouncing back after breathing and believing in another area of life. The point is this: the cycle of *breathe*, *believe*, and *bounce back* tends to come back around and around and around. Each time, you are likely to find yourself quicker to take time to breathe, and you are likely to find that the believing stage is shorter, and you are likely to be even more eager to bounce back and have more specific ideas about what to do and how to proceed. All of that signals spiritual growth in you.

Don't be dismayed at future problems. Rather, be enthusiastic that you know how to respond to them and that you are growing in your trust of the Lord to help you with all manner of difficulty.

Remember this always: you may not *feel* stronger or more spiritually mature . . . but if you have invited the Lord into your situation or pain, He is at work and you are stronger and growing according to His timetable, by His methods, and always in a way that allows Him to bring glory to Himself and rewards to you.

CHAPTER 2

Reclaim Your Lost Time and Opportunity

The time is today. The opportunity is now.
Today and its decisions are God's gifts to you.
—*Anonymous*

Kimberly was forty-six years old when her husband Daryl left her. While she admitted to their marriage having had some rocky moments, she felt "totally surprised" when Daryl went away on a fishing trip one weekend and never came home. Instead she received a copy of papers filing for a divorce. Shortly thereafter all of Daryl's personal possessions and clothing disappeared from their home, and his key to the house was left on the kitchen counter with a little note that said simply, "Sorry, but I have to go."

Kimberly suspected there might be another woman in Daryl's life, but what did it really matter? "We live in a community-property, no-fault-divorce state so it didn't really matter who did what to whom. Daryl was going to have the divorce he wanted."

Initially Kimberly didn't feel very much pain—she was so

angry that she didn't allow herself to feel sorrow. But then a sense of void enveloped her. She said, "I lost so much."

Not only did Kimberly lose her home—Daryl didn't have enough assets to buy out her half of the investment so the house had to be sold—but she lost something she considered to have been a major accomplishment in her life: she had designed the house they shared for twenty-five years and had not only decorated it but had landscaped the property into beautiful gardens and courtyards. The house had been her creation.

Kimberly also said, "I had to go back into the workplace, something I really didn't want to do but had to do in order to support myself financially. I found that much had changed in the twenty years I had not worked outside our home. I did have a small home-based career but it was totally a supplementary job—nothing I could count on to pay all my bills and nothing I could build so that it could become that. Once I got a job, I was overwhelmed with all I needed to learn, or relearn. I felt adrift for months, unsure if I could make it in a world of high-tech, totally computerized processes, competing with women half my age."

A compounding factor: all three of their children seemed to feel more sorry for Daryl than for her. She felt betrayed. "They didn't see their father at fault in this breakup of our family. It isn't that they blamed me, but for whatever reasons—and they couldn't explain their reasons—they saw their father as the one who would have the most difficulty moving on in his life and they felt sad for him. I resented their attitude and, frankly, didn't want to hear *anything* they had to say about their father if it was the least bit positive."

To add to the betrayal, her own brother continued to be friendly with Daryl, even to the point of inviting him to their family events and not inviting Kimberly. "I knew you'd feel uncomfortable," he said. True. But *not* very comforting.

The deepest sense of loss, however, was Kimberly's loss of identity as a woman. She said, "I gave Daryl the best years of my life—my talent, my energy, my love. And what did I get in return? Nothing, really. I was put into a position of having to start over, and with very little energy and self-value. I felt devastated at the thought that, at age forty-six, I had wasted my life in so many ways. I had no companion to share life with, no retirement security, no strong family relationships, and tons of negative feelings, mostly resentment and rejection. I think the rejection was the worst feeling of all. A man I had trusted and with whom I had shared so much *just walked away*. He took my children and my siblings with him. He left me. I was alone with that reality."

It was at that point she felt that "the pain came to the surface. I know I'm bitter—wouldn't *you* be? I know I've got things to work through. I also know that I want justice from God and I'm not sure He's going to give it to me."

In the last ten years, I have met a number of women like Kimberly. The pain is nearly always a pain that *continues* to deepen and to impact their lives. Unless they take action!

Four Great Causes of Emotional Pain

Hurt feelings—perhaps called "damaged emotions," "inner pain," or "emotional turmoil"—frequently arise in a person's life through one of four basic life experiences.

Death and Disease

This is the hurt of *sorrow* that comes in the wake of the death of a loved one—sometimes a spouse, sometimes a child, sometimes a beloved parent. It is also the sorrow that comes as the result of an accident or disease that leaves a person with permanently diminished physical capacity.

Failure

This is the hurt of *error* that comes to us when we make a mistake or commit a sin and find ourselves facing negative consequences for it—which, we must admit, always occur. All choices have consequences and when we make a negative choice we *will* eventually experience a negative consequence. Knowing that doesn't lessen the pain or the severity of the consequence.

Disappointment

This is the hurt of *unmet expectations*. We have dreamed a dream that simply hasn't become a reality, and now we feel it is too late for us to experience the fulfillment we so deeply desired. It may be the failure to marry, to have a child, to win recognition, or to accomplish a goal. We hurt, but generally are reluctant to share fully how deeply we hurt.

Rejection

This the hurt of *abandonment*. Someone we love has walked away from us. It may have been a spouse, a beloved friend, or a business partner. It is likely to be someone we had counted on to be there in our lives, someone we had trusted and in whom we had confided. We are angry at their behavior, but also feel a sense of loss over something valuable that we aren't sure we can recover.

All four of these situations are painful to varying degrees depending on the depth of our dreams, relationships, and the extent to which we feel ourselves at fault. I'm going to describe these four areas in greater detail in just a moment.

Furthermore, all four of these situations are ones that the vast majority of women experience. Not just one of these sources of pain, but *all* of them, come at some point in life, and occasionally several may arrive at the same time!

I personally know what it means to fail, to be disappointed, and to feel rejection. My greatest sense of pain in recent years has been the death of my father. My father was never sick. He was an athlete and a coach. He was a strong believer in Christ, one of the two godliest men I have ever known.

It seemed impossible to us that he was diagnosed with cancer, and that he died from the multiple myeloma that gripped his body.

I prayed so hard.

I believed with all the faith I had.

Others joined me in praying and believing.

It was God's grace that he lived longer than the doctors had originally projected, but in the end my father accomplished all of the things on his list of goals related to his material and financial life. He got the house finished that he was building for my mother, even to the hookup of the gas fireplace. The only thing he did not get to do that he deeply wanted was see his only grandson play baseball—our son, Zach, was only four when his grandfather died.

God also answered our prayers that we could be with my father in the moment of his death. His leave taking was peaceful, even though his body was filled with bone cancer tumors.

It took me several years, however, to come to the point where I knew with absolute certainty that God's plans and purposes for my father were fulfilled. Not necessarily according to what I saw as the purpose for his life, but what *God* saw. God doesn't waste a wound. He doesn't back away from His promises.

I still miss my father . . . a lot. Even to the point of tears. But I also believe with all my heart that God has him doing things that are even now part of God's ongoing greater plans and purposes for his life.

**We may never know *why* certain things happen,
but God knows, and we can know Him!**

I was like most people I know—I asked God why a thousand times. He didn't tell me. But I came to know two things:

We may never know why certain things happen, but God knows, and we can know Him! God never asks that we know or understand everything. He asks that we trust Him.

Plus, God does use loss to teach us amazing lessons about His love, mercy, and grace. And these lessons, if we will choose to learn them, make us stronger, wiser, and more effective for Christ.

The General Process of Dealing with Loss

Certain basic principles seem to be related to all forms of loss. What applies to one form tends to apply to other forms.

The Loss Experienced with Death and Disease

Death is a major loss, but the loss is not limited to physical death. We can experience the death of our own self-perception (as being perfect, accomplished, or "on track"), the death of a dream, or the death of a relationship. There is a finality to major loss that we don't feel if we intuitively sense that a loss is minor or transient. If we lose our cell phone, we know it can be replaced. If we lose a beloved employee, we still have a sense that we might hire someone new to take her place. If we crash the mainframe computer at work with something we did in data entry, we can trust that somebody can fix the computer and we might learn how *not* to do whatever it is we did! It is when we have a major loss that we also have a sense there isn't anything we can personally do to "fix" what happened or to restore a loss of function.

In the case of actual death, there is a grieving process we must work through before we can bounce back. The basic process does include breathing—taking time to mourn and heal. For most people, there is a degree of believing—we often find ourselves asking, "Why didn't God prevent this?" or "Why would a loving heavenly Father allow this to happen?" These questions call our believing into question.

On the one hand, the answers to these questions are ones we cannot know, at least not fully in this lifetime. The greater truth is that we rarely *need* to know fully why God does what He does or why He allows what He allows. We can know with certainty that God loves us and that He cares for us in our sorrow—deeply and tenderly—and that God has a purpose for all that He does even if we don't see or understand that purpose. There is *something* that God desires for us to learn, do, or say in the midst of our grief that can help others, and when we help others, help comes back to us when we need it most and in the form we most need.

As part of the grieving process, we *must* continue to believe that God is good. He is faithful and loving. He is utterly trust-worthy. And He is forever in relationship with us, seeking to produce in us those attributes that will bring us to eternal reward and earthly blessing!

We face a challenge to reaffirm these truths relating to our believing when we experience loss.

Bouncing back after the death of someone or something important to us generally means that we earnestly seek and grab hold of two things: a way of coping with the loss that leads us to peace and joy, and finding a new outlet for love.

Coping with a loss can mean a new prosthetic device or strength regained through rehabilitation. It can mean learning how to live with new medications or required therapies—and making the most of a doctor's waiting room.

Beverly was an inspiration to me in this. She told me that she still sees three doctors in the aftermath of a stroke she experienced a couple of years ago. She said, "At times I feel as if I am spending a significant amount of my time in the doctors' waiting rooms. So I have a little satchel that I've filled with waiting-room things to do. I have a small piece of needlework—at present, it's yarn to make a baby's blanket that I will give to the homeless shelter connected with my church. I have a few pieces of stationery and envelopes and some stamps and my address book so I can catch up on thank-you notes and notes of encouragement. I have a small Bible and a small notepad. I usually have a paperback book that is inspirational. And whenever possible, I put all these things aside and strike up a conversation with another person in the waiting room. Often my knitting is the impetus for a conversation. I have found that more than half the time I have an opportunity in these conversations to share Christ with a person and perhaps even pray with someone. In a couple of instances, I have forged a relationship that turned into a periodic lunch or tea time together."

She went on to say, "I thought when I had my stroke that I had lost far more than I could ever recover. I think right now, two years out, I have *gained* more than I could ever have imagined!"

Beverly's life is *not* a replica of her life before her stroke. It is a bounce-back life that is fulfilling and meaningful, even in the physicians' waiting rooms. She has new opportunities to help people, and in that she finds purpose and fulfillment. She is even considering volunteering at an elder-care center that specializes in caregiver-relief programs for those helping family members who have had strokes.

The Loss That Comes with Failure

In many cases, we can recover at least part of what we lose when we suffer a personal failure. We might get another job, take on another challenge and succeed in it, or win the next audition. But there are some forms of failure that are extremely difficult to face and overcome. The failure cuts off or alters all of life's potential in a certain area, or negates a sense of purpose.

When Kara and Kevin lost their daughter to suicide, they experienced more than a normal grieving process at the death of their beloved child. They both felt a profound sense of failure. "We kept asking ourselves," Kara said, "what we had missed. Why didn't we sense how depressed Sissy had become? Why didn't others around her tell us what they were witnessing in her—especially since we saw her so infrequently given the fact that she had moved several hundred miles away? Where were her church friends when she needed church friends the most?"

Kevin added, "We asked ourselves why a young woman who loved the Lord with such an open and fresh witness would take this step. We had a deep sense that we had failed our daughter as parents."

Kara and Kevin admitted that they fell into a downward spiral of tears and never-ending *why* and *what if* questions. "Then one day," Kara said, "we looked at each other and said, 'We need to stop rehashing all these old questions.' We made a decision to take a short cruise to someplace warm and beautiful that we had never experienced before. We found that almost immediately after we boarded the ship, we gave in to great feelings of exhaustion. We had worn ourselves out emotionally. We slept and slept and slept."

Kevin added, "We only seemed to emerge from our cabin for meals. Fortunately, we had a balcony outside our cabin and we often slept in those lounge chairs! Forget the shore excursions."

"The good news," Kara concluded, "is that we came home rested for the first time in more than a year. On the cruise we decided that each day we would read the Scriptures aloud to each other. We didn't really discuss them. We just read. It was soothing and healing."

Kara and Kevin had combined both breathing and believing in a very wonderful way!

And what about bouncing back?

This couple realized they could not do anything to bring back their daughter, but they could keep her memory alive. Kevin refinished all of her old bedroom furniture and Kara redecorated the guest room in their vacation home in her memory, and they began to invite other couples who had lost children to death—often SIDS babies or those who had late-term miscarriages—to come to their home by the lake and stay in

"Sissy's Room" for a long weekend of pampering. Kara and Kevin listened to their guests, served them gourmet meals, and gave them plenty of space to rest and walk the numerous paths on their property. They had prayer times with these bereaved parents and encouraged them in their faith.

Kara and Kevin hadn't counted on having a ministry, but they do have one. It is a quiet, private ministry of love and encouragement in Christ. They only host guests once every month to six weeks—more frequent hosting was a little debilitating to them both. "We need time between guests to fuel our own encouragement and to renew our own souls," said Kara. "A person has to 'take in' in order to be able to 'give out.'" Rather than dredge up memories of their own grief, which they had initially feared might happen, they have found it very therapeutic to admit their personal flaws and point to Christ Jesus as the source of their strength and help.

The Loss Associated with Disappointment

Norma said to me, "I felt that I had wasted a full five years on a man who didn't turn out at all to be the man I thought he was. He kept making promises to me that he never acted upon. And rather than confront him about this, I swallowed my suspicions, hurt, and anger and continued to be sweet, loving, and accommodating.

"I was hoping, of course, that he would marry me as he had said he *wanted* to, and that his reluctance to do this had been related to outward circumstances beyond his control: a fire at his business, a lack of finances, a concern over the health of his parents—things that all made sense. I had absolutely no idea he was lying to me. I don't think I was blind to the possibility he might be lying as much as I was in love with a man who was a very, very, very good liar!"

One day the truth came out. Her dream guy, Bill, was already married. He and his wife had been separated for several years, but they were still legally married. In truth, he had been married from the first day Norma met him. "I was in shock. I had no idea that there was another woman in his life, much less a *wife*. And there was more shock to come. He admitted that the problem in his marriage was a problem he still had: he was struggling with homosexual urges and even had taken a male lover on two occasions. Those had not been one-night stands but ongoing affairs that lasted two to eight months. I was devastated and just kept thanking God that I had purposefully chosen to remain celibate in our relationship."

Did Norma breathe? Yes, indeed. She took two weeks off from work and moved to a nearby city. She paused often as she unpacked and settled in to spend time with the Lord, sometimes in tears, but with her Bible in hand. She was determined to stay in touch with Christian friends. Bill had not gone to church with her regularly so she felt no need to change her church affiliation, and since she parted ways with Bill, she hasn't seen him at church. She considers that a real blessing.

Did Norma continue to believe? "Oh, yes!" she said. "I had a strong sense that God had spared me from what could have been a terrible future. But I also had to question myself, 'What has been my fault in this? Why didn't I sense God nudging me to end the relationship?'"

Norma finally concluded two things. "First," she said, "I realized I had so desperately wanted to be married that I had blinded myself to any spiritual or emotional flaws in Bill. I saw him as my knight in shining armor." And then she laughed as she added, "When in truth, there was mud everywhere on that armor!" She asked God to open her eyes and help her to not be deceived in the future.

"Second," she said, "I concluded that I needed to focus on what God might want to do in me and what He might want me to do with my life even if I never get married."

Norma began to spend more time daily in reading and studying the Bible and in prayer. She went to a number of retreats on various topics—some of them work oriented, some spiritually oriented. She said, "I experienced new levels of God's presence and I came away not only with a strong affirmation of my own faith in God, but a strong affirmation *from* God that He loved me and that He had never forsaken me and never would forsake me."

Norma bounced back! She became involved in an outreach to unwed mothers at a Christ-centered pregnancy center. "It wasn't exactly the place I ever expected to meet a guy to date," she said, "but I did."

A man brought his fourteen-year-old daughter to the center. She had been living with her aunt in a nearby state because he was a truck driver and wasn't at home with the consistency he felt she needed in a parent. The daughter had made a one-time, one-night mistake and was seeking help in deciding whether to have an abortion or give her baby up for adoption.

"We had a number of wonderful conversations and then I didn't see this man for several months." His daughter had her baby and gave it to a loving couple in an open-adoption arrangement. He had been dealing personally with his own sense of loss and failure, and his dashed hopes for a grandchild. He reached out to Norma "as the kindest and godliest woman I've met in the last two years." They are still getting to know each other, but of two things Norma is certain: he isn't married (his wife died several years ago) and he isn't gay.

From Norma's viewpoint, she is glad that she isn't "out of her mind" in her love for this man. She said, "Both of my feet are on the ground—or perhaps I should say both of my knees are on the ground in prayer before the Lord. I'm asking lots of questions, taking things slowly, and staying in the Scriptures daily. I truly don't feel like the same woman who once dated a guy named Bill. I have changed in good ways and I can feel myself growing spiritually. I'm not expecting any man to meet all of my needs. Rather, I'm seeking new ways I might be able to help a man as a true helpmeet in a marriage. That's a major shift for me."

For Cindy, dashed hopes came fairly early in her life. She

had gone to college and had studied theatre arts as her major. After college, she went to New York City to take acting classes. She auditioned, auditioned, and auditioned. She got a few minor parts. "I was on stage for four minutes in one off-Broadway play, which opened and closed in four nights! I was in a total of forty-eight seconds of TV commercials and on soap operas as a walk-on extra who had no lines. I had more than a sense of failure. I had a sense that I would never be the actress I had always aspired to be."

Cindy went back to school and got her teaching certification so she could teach at the high-school level—not acting, but English literature, which had been her second love. She said, "After I returned home from New York, I needed a break. I worked at a summer camp as a cook. I was too busy to wallow in self-pity. For me, this was *breathing*."

She added, "The camp was a church camp so I had plenty of opportunity to hear sermons and have conversations with my coworkers about our mutual faith in Christ. I realized that my relationship with the Lord had grown a bit cool while I was in the City. It was renewed at camp as I came to grips with what I truly believe about Jesus: He does have a plan for my life. I memorized Jeremiah 29:11–14 that summer and it still is a verse that I say to myself almost every day: '"For I know the plans I have for you," declares the LORD, "plans to prosper you and not to harm you, plans to give you hope and a future. Then you will call on me and come and pray to me, and I will listen to you. You will seek me and find me when you seek me with all your heart.

I will be found by you."' That's what I believed, and it's what I continue to believe."

After she had been teaching high school for a couple of years, Cindy got involved in the drama ministry at her church, and she finds great enjoyment in participating in skits that are sometimes performed in place of a sermon on Sunday evenings. "The funny thing is that I don't think of myself as an actress," Cindy said. "I think of myself as a minister, and the net result is probably that I'm a much better actress than when I was pursuing that career!"

The Loss Associated with Rejection

I believe being rejected is the greatest hit that most women can take and still live. As one woman said, "Rejection knocked me for a loop—I could hardly get out of bed on some days. Memories would hit me and send me reeling."

In many ways, there are elements of rejection involved in death. Many widows admit to feeling that their husbands abandoned them even when they know rationally that there isn't anything they *could* have done to keep their husband alive. A failure can leave a person feeling as if something inside them died in the process. The loss of a dream is sometimes described as the *death* of a dream.

Rejection, for our purposes here, is when a person you love turns away from you—regardless of anything you may have done or not done. They have simply chosen to walk out of your life. Their action is intentional. The person may not realize he or she has inflicted as much harm as has been rendered, but the act of "leaving you behind" or of "walking in a new direction" is an act of their conscious will.

One of the people in the Bible who certainly knew a great deal about rejection was Leah, the son of a man named Laban. Her aunt was Rebekah, the wife of Isaac. She became Jacob's first wife. Rachel was her sister.

Yes, *that* Leah.

Few of us have ever experienced ongoing rejection in the way Leah did.

The Bible tells us that Jacob ran to Uncle Laban's home after he had tricked his older twin brother, Esau, out of both the family inheritance and their father's blessing. Esau had let it be known that he intended to kill Jacob after Isaac, their father, died. Jacob literally ran for his life. And once at Laban's home, he almost immediately fell in love with Laban's daughter Rachel, who is one of only a few women described in the Bible as being attractive in form and beautiful. In other words, she had lovely facial features and a great figure (Genesis 29:17).

Jacob agreed to work for Laban for seven years to win Rachel's hand in marriage. His love for Rachel was so deep that those years seemed to go by quickly. At the end of seven years, a festive week-long wedding was planned, with plenty of drink to go along with it. The bride, heavily veiled, went through the ceremony and occupied the bridal chamber where the marriage was consummated. And then, to Jacob's horror and Leah's chagrin, the ruse of Laban came to light the morning *after* the wedding. The bride had been Leah, not Rachel.

Laban argued that it was the custom for an elder daughter to be married before a younger daughter could be given in marriage. He agreed to give Rachel to Jacob—for another seven years of servitude on his estate. And Jacob agreed.

I was grateful to learn just a few years ago that Jacob didn't have to work fourteen years before he could marry Rachel. She likely was given to him in marriage just a week or two after the wedding between Jacob and Leah. But the ongoing work for Laban meant another seven years before Jacob had paid in full the bridal dowry.

What an awkward situation this must have been for both young women. Rachel ended up sexually sharing her beloved Jacob with her older sister! And imagine the pain for Leah—married to a man who didn't love her, keeping "house" in a tent adjacent to her sister's tent.

Rejection and abandonment often *feel* identical.

I truly believe that Leah had felt rejection—abandonment at a very deep level—from her father long before she felt it from Jacob. Rejection and abandonment often *feel* identical.

There is no mention in the Bible that Laban did *anything* to find a husband for Leah (other than Jacob). The Bible describes Leah as having "weak eyes." Bible scholars have thought this might mean that she was permanently cross-eyed or that she had a wandering eye. Either way, this was not a trait of beauty.

There is no mention of her character or personality—only a flaw. Laban may very well have been guilty of a trait that a fairly high percentage of fathers have: they love one daughter more than another.

As for Jacob, he fulfilled his obligation as a husband to Leah, but there is no mention at all that he spoke to her or about her with affection. In fact, there's only one statement of conversation that we find in the Bible between Leah and Jacob. Leah said to Jacob one evening as he came in from the fields, "You must sleep with me. I have hired you with my son's mandrakes" (Genesis 30:16). (Leah's son had gathered this plant, considered an aphro-disiac, and Leah had sold the plant to Rachel. She preempted Rachel's use of the plant, however, by insisting that Jacob fulfill his conjugal obligations. Not exactly the stuff of romance.)

Leah knew Jacob's rejection *all* her married life. Even after she had borne Jacob four sons and a daughter, and her maidser-vants had borne two sons to Jacob (which legally were considered Leah's sons), Jacob made it very clear that his preferred wife and confidante was Rachel.

Leah faithfully followed Jacob when he finally left Laban's home. She gave up all that she knew as culture, family stability, and a home base. In many ways, she was alone in the midst of a crowd—which is the way that many women feel if they are living with or have experienced rejection.

What can we learn from Leah?

I believe the great lesson from her to all women who experience loss of any kind is this: God *will* overcome loss and ensure us that we *will* have all that He has planned and purposed for us! We must claim all that God says is ours to have.

Claiming What God Says Is Yours

Leah's eight sons (six from her womb and two from her maidservant Zilpah) were two-thirds of the "twelve tribes of Israel." The Bible tells us repeatedly that God looked with favor on Leah. Jacob may have preferred Rachel, but God remained faithful to Leah in spite of Jacob's rejection.

If you are feeling rejected today, recognize that your rejection is at the hands of a human being. *God* has not rejected you! You are still His beloved daughter and He has many acts of favor to bestow on you.

How did Leah cope? I believe she did three things that are vital for every woman to do in the face of loss.

Leah Fully Embraced What She *Did* Have

Leah had six sons and a daughter, plus two "foster sons" to raise. And she did this living a nomadic life, very likely spending most of her married life in a tent. She had meals to fix, a home to clean and care for, and no doubt an endless round of squabbles to referee and lessons of character to impart to her children. She may not have had the romance in her life that she desired, but she did have responsibilities that needed her time, energy, and continual attention.

I also believe that Leah did receive a great deal of affection in her life—perhaps *more* affection in the totality of her life than her sister, Rachel, received. We sometimes think of little boys as being aloof, distant, uncaring. But in my experience, I find that little boys very often have a much stronger emotional attachment to their mothers than to their fathers and often have an ongoing strong emotional attachment to Mom to a greater degree than their sisters do. Mom is the first woman in the life of a little boy and is nearly always a major influence.

Leah had lots of children to hug and nurture and tuck into bed at night. She had lots of skinned knees to kiss and wounds to heal. Leah became a woman who very likely embraced the affection she *did* receive from her children.

Leah Saw Her Children as God's Gift

Leah named each of her children and, in doing so, voiced praise to God for them. About her firstborn, Reuben, she said, "Surely the Lord has seen my misery." The name *Reuben* has literally been assigned the meaning, "Behold, a son!" Leah saw Reuben as a gift from *God*, not a gift from Jacob.

About her second son, Simeon, she said the Lord had given him to her "because the Lord heard that I am not loved." She believed the Lord's gift of this son was a gift of God's love and God's *awareness* of Leah's circumstances. The name *Simeon* means "hearing," which tells us that Leah may very well have believed God had heard her cries of sadness in the night hours.

When her third son, Levi, was born, she saw this child as a validation of her role as a wife and made a faith statement: "Now at last my husband will become attached to me." Levi's name means "joined." Although things did not turn out exactly as Leah had perhaps hoped, the birth of this third son, which fully established her as a wife, was perceived by her as a sign that God believed she was fully Jacob's wife. (Note: the descendants of Abraham had a longstanding belief that God's favor was established by the presence of two or more witnesses. This was long before the Law of Moses expressed this belief.)

Levi, of course, was the ancestor of Moses and Aaron. The Levites were the chief administrators of the spiritual life and rituals that God established for His people. Leah was entrusted with the spiritual formation and development of this son—a profound role for every woman who believes her child is destined for service in God's kingdom!

About Leah's fourth son, she said, "This time I will praise the Lord." The implication seems to be that Leah had given up trying to win Jacob's favor and had devoted herself primarily to her relationship with the Lord. For many women, this is the place to which God is calling them after they experience rejection. They begin to see their life as a daughter of the Most High God, a role far above and beyond any earthly relationship. Even women who are deeply loved and have good marriages have told me that they came to a place of spiritual maturity in which they regarded themselves first and foremost as a "daughter of the Lord." That role is one filled with reward and satisfaction!

Leah named her fourth son Judah, which means "praise." Judah was the ancestor of King David and ultimately of Jesus. God had entrusted Leah with the leadership potential of this boy—and with instilling in him the character traits that led him to confront his older brother Reuben and insist that Joseph's life be spared even when Reuben wanted Joseph to be killed.

After giving birth to four sons, Leah gave her maidservant Zilpah to Jacob to see if God would favor her with more children. Sure enough, Zilpah had a son that Leah named Gad. In naming him, she took him fully as her son to raise. The name *Gad* means "good fortune." Then Zilpah had a second son and Leah named him Asher, saying, "How happy I am!" His name has come to mean "happy."

Leah had a fifth son named Issachar, which she regarded as a reward from the Lord for having given Zilpah to Jacob so she might bear children. The name *Issachar* means "reward."

And finally, Leah gave birth to a sixth son that she named Zebulun, saying, "God has presented me with a precious gift." The name *Zebulun* means "dwelling" or "abiding place." The implication is that this sixth son gave Leah a deep sense of permanence, honor, and stability.

Perhaps as icing on the cake—at least in the eyes of many women—Leah gave birth to a daughter she named Dinah. The Bible tells us this happened "some time later." Dinah may very well have been the baby who was born long after Leah *stopped* trying to have children. It does happen!

Overall, there seems to be a spiritual progression in Leah's statements about her sons. She went from a position of seeing her sons as a sign from God that her marriage was valid to a position of praise for a son being a God-sent gift. She began to exhibit an awareness of God's good fortune and happiness. And ultimately, Leah seems to have become so established in her relationship with the Lord that she regarded all things associated with her life as a reward. Her self-value was firmly rooted in God's love.

Something often overlooked in the life of Leah is that she became stepmother to her sister's children. Rachel had her son Joseph *after* the birth of all Leah's children, including Dinah. It was in giving birth to her second son, Benjamin, that Rachel died. These two boys, Joseph and Benjamin, were orphaned at very young ages. Rachel had a maidservant named Biljah, but she is never described as anything other than the mother of Dan and Naphtali—sons she bore to Jacob at Rachel's command. The strong mother figure in the camp of Jacob would have been Leah. And she no doubt had a profound influence on Joseph and Benjamin.

Leah Did Not Waste Emotional Energy on Anger

One of my favorite quotes about anger is a statement made by Ralph Waldo Emerson. He said, "For every minute you are angry you lose sixty seconds of happiness." Leah didn't waste time on anger, which would have resolved nothing in her life.

In reading about Leah, we can sense disappointment and longing in her, but there is no behavior that speaks of rebellion or seething anger. She showed no signs of plotting revenge. Indeed, it was Rachel who stole the family idols—indicative of a right to inherit family wealth—from their father, Laban. Leah willingly loaded up her family and her life and went with Jacob back to Canaan when Jacob felt the time had come to return home. Leah did not *insist* that Jacob give her anything, as Rachel did—apparently with great anguish. While Leah did stand up for her conjugal rights, she did not speak in a jealous rage to Jacob, as Rachel did, saying, "Give me children, or I'll die!" (See Genesis 29 and 30 for these stories about Leah and Rachel.)

Three Responses to Loss and Rejection

Leah gives us a strong example of the three things we are wise to do any time we experience loss, especially loss coupled with rejection.

Embrace What *Is* Rather Than Focus on What *Isn't*

Fully involve yourself with the people and opportunities God is giving to you now, and move forward. Don't dwell on what might have been or what you wish would be.

Turn to God, Not Away from Him

As one woman once said, "I chose to burrow into God." Spend more time with the Lord and in His Word. See the Lord as the *primary* source of love in your life. His presence is not just for today and tomorrow—it is everlasting.

Refuse to Give In to Any Negative Emotion

Just say no to hate, resentment, bitterness, and anger. These emotions do not produce *anything* positive in a person's life, not now and not in the future.

"But I need to vent," you may be saying to yourself.

Well . . . vent thanksgiving and praise for what God *has* done for you and for who God is now and forever!

"But I have a good cause to be angry or bitter," you may be saying.

The truth is, no cause is good enough justification for stopping the flow of God's mercy and love moving through you to others. Nothing clogs a woman's soul as much as anger or bitterness. Nothing thwarts a woman's ability to be used by God as much as personal hatred or feelings of vengeance.

Lay down the negative so you can pick up the positive. Put off the pain and put on the love of the Lord!

I realize that many of the women who come to our Extraordinary Women conferences will return home to the very problems they were seeking to escape for a few days. Sometimes we can do very little to change our circumstances. Sometimes we can do very little to change or influence others around us.

But we can do something about ourselves! The most important person you can change or influence is the woman who looks back at you from your own mirror.

Never a Complete Loss of Time or Opportunity

You may *feel* as if you have lost time or opportunity. You may *feel* as if you have wasted your energy and resources on something that has brought you a very meager return on your investment.

The greater truth is this: in God's eyes, no child of His *ever* loses time or opportunity.

God has all eternity awaiting you.

God has opportunities ahead that you cannot begin to imagine in this present moment.

The most important person you can change or influence is the woman who looks back at you from your own mirror.

The Bible promises us that God alone can turn *all* things to a good end in the lives of those who love Him and seek to follow Him (Romans 8:28). God can take even the biggest and most painful losses of our life and weave them into the fabric of our future in a way that brings beauty to our witness, the warmth of love to others in need, and a restoration of esteem to those who feel as if they have been stripped naked in the public square. What you see as a tragic reduction of your life, God sees as an opportunity to rebuild what might truly become the new and improved you.

CHAPTER 3

Overcome Your Exhaustion and Stress

You can't get the water to clear up until
you get the pigs out of the creek.
—*Hillbilly saying*

A wise elderly woman once said to me, "Honey, let me tell you a beauty secret that few women seem to know."

I was all ears. This woman had skin that was flawless, and even though she must have been in her seventies, she had a glow and vibrancy about her that made a person see her and respond to her as if she was thirty.

"Tell me!" I responded.

"Stress makes you tired and wrinkled. And tired and wrinkled come across as old and ugly."

She thought this insight might help me in my work with women's conferences. In truth, her insight helped *me*! I made a renewed commitment to live a stress-limited life.

Another woman once said, "Stress is an inside job." Simply stated, but no less profound.

I was thinking about what these two women told me in years past and it suddenly came clear: we have all been taught at some point in our life that "beauty comes from the inside." We all know and have admired women who had a high degree of inner beauty.

Well, stress is definitely something that hits a woman's inner beauty. Anxiety, worry, and having too much to do in too little time can put a woman on an unending treadmill that not only tires her body but exhausts her supply of joy. Stress is *directly* related to all things that make a woman

- too tired to set new goals and dream new dreams;
- too focused on tasks, without enough "people" or "personal" time—the result nearly always being a decline in relationships that matter the most;
- too preoccupied with details that are temporary—which limits a woman's insights into the broader and more important perspectives of eternity and long-range fulfillment.

Stress drains us as few things can.

Stress is not only depleting. It is painful. There is a literal ache that comes with exhaustion that is not resolved. I have a friend who has told me on several occasions that she can only go for twenty hours and about twenty minutes before her entire body begins to hurt, from the top of her head to her toes. She says, "This is a signal that I've gone way past the end." I'm not sure I could go twenty hours.

The cure for stress is not all that complicated. A person generally has to do one of these things:

- Remove something from life's agenda.

- Remove a responsibility from life's demands.

- Decide that perfection is not possible, completion is admirable, and self-forgiveness is required.

What might you need to eliminate from your agenda? What responsibilities might you need to delegate? Are you willing to trade in perfectionism for completionism?

The Exhaustion of Trying to Have It All

For decades we have been told that as women we can have it all. Not long ago a woman said to me, "I'm in my sixties now and I've learned that a woman *can* have it all . . . just not all at the same time." By "all," most refer to a career, a family, and personal fulfillment.

Those who seek to have it all nearly always find themselves cutting corners in one area of life in order to accommodate another. Balance is critical and very difficult to establish and sustain. The balancing act seems to have a built-in exhaustion factor.

The need for balance in life includes relaxation. High-energy days require sleep. Creativity requires relaxed time for daydreaming. Intense relationships seem to require more personal time for processing, evaluating, and nurturing than casual acquaintances.

We often see the need for balance when one of the opposites of a whole—such as rest and productivity—falls below the level that is sufficient. Sleep-deprived people are less productive and often more accident-prone, which can lead to an injury that results in *no* productivity!

The sad fact is that women who pursue it "all" tend to short-change themselves. They give to husbands and children and careers, and then find nothing left over to fuel their own souls. They've forgotten what they've heard on every airline flight: "Put on your own oxygen mask before you attempt to help someone seated next to you"!

Exhaustion from Doing Too Much

Have you ever been too exhausted to even think about being exhausted? Perhaps you are thinking that *nothing* sounds as good as a hundred-year nap and then awakening as Rip Van Winkle did to find a whole new world filled with fun new technologies and people.

When I shared this idea of a hundred-year nap with a small group of women, one of them said to me later, "Julie, I'd just settle for a hundred *minutes* of uninterrupted sleep!"

"Tell me about your day," I said.

Shondra recounted in lockstep detail all that had been on her plate during the last twenty-four-hour period.

She had awakened to a 5:30 a.m. alarm after four hours of sleep, with brief times awake after her first and second hours of sleep. She got dressed quickly and finished preparation of a major proposal she was pitching later that day to key corporate clients. She made sack lunches for her two children, took time to walk on her treadmill in their family room for twenty minutes, made herself a protein shake, and woke her husband. Then she called to the children, and while they were getting up she dressed and made breakfast for the family, which was consumed in about five minutes at the kitchen counter. While they were eating, she cleaned up the dishes and the entire family was out the door by seven thirty to beat the traffic.

She dropped their two children at their respective schools about two miles apart and eight miles from their home, and then drove in the opposite direction to her office, where she put in a nine-hour nonstop day of staff meetings, telephone calls, an international conference call, and the one-hour presentation to a client. Everything about her workday seemed "urgent" and "vital" and "demanding."

After the major client presentation, there was a round of debriefing meetings. Right before walking into her office in the morning, she had grabbed a quick sandwich at a small shop next door to her office building. She consumed this sandwich at her desk while double tasking at writing memos and checking her e-mail inbox, which had 197 messages awaiting her between eight o'clock and noon.

At 5:15 p.m. she left her office, picked up the children from after-school day care, made quick stops at the dry cleaner and gas station, and stopped for a five-minute run into the grocery store to get a loaf of bread, two quarts of milk, and bananas. When she got home, she started dinner, then sat down with the children to walk through their homework assignments. She put in a load of laundry and folded a second load that had finished drying the evening before. She sorted the mail and listened with one ear to her answering machine, returned a call to her mother to answer a question that seemed urgent, and also caught up on the national news and local weather. She let out the dog and replenished his water bowl and put food in his dish.

After eating a quick dinner, she turned over the "finish up homework" chore to her husband and sat down to read a seventy-eight-page report to which she needed to submit a response to her executive supervisor by ten o'clock the next morning. She wrote an e-mail to a client in Japan, and when he surprised her with a return phone call, she talked with him for about twenty minutes to answer several questions and give him the assurance that her company *could* meet the deadline proposed to him. She added to me at this point, "I don't know *how* we will meet the deadline, but we *will*."

She tucked her son into bed. She then sat down on the edge of her daughter's bed to have a brief conversation with her about the kind of dress she wanted to shop for and the gift she might want to buy—both related to a fairly formal birthday-party invitation.

She had a brief conversation with her husband about whether they should allow their daughter to quit piano lessons (voicing their mutual sadness that she didn't seem to have much innate musical ability) and encourage their son to trade in track-team practice for marching band (because he *did* have musical ability and not a lot of potential at pole vaulting).

While taking a bath, she made a preliminary outline for the response she needed to write, and then began a draft of the response while sitting up in bed until midnight, at which point she said, "My eyes wouldn't focus anymore."

She paused at that point and I jumped in with, "I think you managed to cram twenty-nine hours of activity into twenty-four hours, not counting sleep."

Shondra replied with weariness and resignation, "I know I should have spent more time with the Lord in prayer and reading God's Word, but frankly, I didn't have time to think about taking time."

Just listening to her schedule gave me a tightening in *my* stomach—I had no difficulty imagining the level of stress she felt or the degree of exhaustion that she was experiencing.

Not long ago I recounted Shondra's daily routine and asked a small group of women if they could relate to her. I said, "Even if you don't have the corporate job Shondra has, do your days seemed marked by racing to get everything done?"

Every hand in the room went up.

I then asked, "Do you have a feeling *right now* of exhaustion at the core of your soul?"

Again, every hand in the room was raised.

I asked a third question. "Is this the way you want to live?"

I saw many shake their heads slowly in a silent no.

So what did Shondra do?

Well, at first she did *not* take my advice—which was to separate from her life for a short while just to breathe. When I suggested this, Shondra said immediately, "I don't have any time for that." I've discovered that most overbooked, overextended women are highly reluctant to do the one thing that will help them the most: step back from their lives for a few days to rest and reflect.

Eventually Shondra did take a few days away. A stubborn sinus infection drove her to it. She agreed with her husband that she would take four days of alone time, and then she would watch the children and hold down the home front while he took a four-day fishing trip with his buddies.

Shondra told me later, "I didn't know how out of breath I had been until I went away to breathe. I slept for ten hours straight the first day I was away. And then I reintroduced myself to God."

"You did *what*?" I asked.

"I felt so out of sync in my relationship with the Lord that I needed to humbly come before Him and ask His forgiveness for my being AWOL. I experienced a wonderful sense of His presence—it was an hour that stands out among all the others. I found myself saying again and again, 'Yes, Lord, I *do* love You. Yes, Lord, I *do* want what You want for me. Yes, Lord, I *do* want to make the changes that will keep me closer to You and help me walk through this life with greater grace, ease, and peace.'" She added, "I don't know if that's what you have in mind for *believe*, but I realized the more I voiced statements such as these to the Lord, the more I was getting back in touch with what I truly believe and value."

On her last day away from the routine of her life, Shondra made a list that she labeled "Moving-Forward Priorities." She said, "I found ways that I could make some adjustments to the daily routine. Just as one little example, I decided that I'd let my seven-year-old son and ten-year-old daughter make their own sandwiches and pack their own sack lunches. I made a decision that I would get done at work what I could do, but on at least three nights a week, I would *not* bring work home. Those nights would be my time to catch up on personal reading and mail. Little things. But they added up to hours and also a greater sense of balance. I also decided that at least one weekend night, my husband and I are going to go out on a date. We've always thought that was a good idea but we never thought we had the time. Well, we're going to hire a yard man and a handyman so we *do* have the time!"

Shondra already had a new bounce in her step when we talked. She was the embodiment of bounce-back enthusiasm for her own future.

Exhaustion from Caring Too Much

Most people believe that "caring" is an important manifestation of a Christian faith walk. As women, we seem to have a built-in drive to nurture—especially our children. Most women, however, have never considered the possibility that a person can care too much. In certain circles, this is now drawing attention for scientific studies—the phenomenon is called *overcaring*.

The person who overcares tends to do several things:

- Take on responsibilities that another person can and should do for their own benefit.

- Be present to a person twenty-four hours a day, every day of the year.

- See their role in the other person's life as indispensable and irreplaceable.

The truth, however, is that God designed us to care but not overcare.

Iris was the primary caregiver for her elderly mother for twelve years, during which time her mother was diagnosed with Alzheimer's. Although Iris had two sisters, they lived more than fifty miles away. Iris, who was divorced without children, was perceived as "having the time" to care for Mom. The full burden of care fell on Iris' shoulders.

Iris did an excellent job of caring for her mother's every need, including moving her into her home so she could be available to her mother twenty-four hours a day. She nearly put herself into the hospital along the way.

One day, Iris' pastor came to the home she shared with her mother and asked, "Iris, who is helping you take care of your mother?"

Iris burst into tears, unable to speak. She said later, "That one question changed my life. I hadn't realized my tears and exhaustion were so near the surface. When I was finally able to speak, I replied, 'Nobody.'" My pastor said, 'Let's make a change in that and ask God to help you follow through on what we decide this afternoon.'"

Iris and her pastor mapped out a plan. It included, first, a week for Iris to go away on a little trip. Think *breathe*! During that week, Iris' mother went to an Alzheimer's nursing facility that allowed for temporary respite care. During the week away, Iris agreed that she would give some thought to what *she* needed in her life—in other words, her own personal needs that were going unmet. The pastor gave her a short list of Bible passages to read. The foremost verses he gave to her were these:

- "Carry each other's burdens, and in this way you will fulfill the law of Christ" (Galatians 6:2).
- "Each one should carry their own load" (Galatians 6:5).

"Those verses sound like they refer to the same load of burdens, don't they?" the pastor asked. Iris nodded in agreement.

"The problem we have is that both of these verses use words that are similar in English but very different in Greek, which is the language in which the New Testament letters of Paul were written. The first verse refers to a burden that is like a huge pile of rocks that have slid down a mountainside and engulfed a person. The person is trying to dig out of the rockslide and stand up with a big boulder on her back. Paul advised that a group of people—or the church as a whole—help lift and carry such a burden until the person is able to regain her health, balance, and strength. Paul wrote this in a spiritual context, using it as an illustration for the way we are to help our brothers and sisters in Christ become free of the burdens of evil and sin that tend to engulf us and weigh us down.

"The second verse," the pastor explained, "refers to a little knapsack in which a person might have collected a few rocks. Paul advised a person to deal with her own load of little rocks whenever possible. We are not to attempt to unburden a person of problems that she acquires through her own choices and behavior. For many people, like you, problems can be God's way of forcing us to confront our own behavior, or to learn how to use our faith in new and more effective ways."

Problems can be God's way of forcing us to confront our own behavior, or to learn how to use our faith in new and more effective ways.

Iris felt as if someone had turned on a light. She said, "So, I may actually be hindering God's work in my mother and in the lives of my sisters by taking on *all* the responsibility for Mom?"

"You may be," the pastor said. "I encourage you to talk to God about this, and as you pray while on your vacation, I hope you will ask the Lord to reveal to you again *His* plan and purpose for *your* life. I suspect He may reveal to you things that He desires for you to do that are currently going undone— things of joy and peace. Remember that Jesus said, 'My yoke is easy, and my burden is light' (Matthew 11:30). Jesus calls us to works that fulfill us and excite us. He never calls us to take on stress and obligations that totally deplete us or wipe the smile off our face."

Iris spent time on her vacation soaking up the natural beauty of one of the most scenic drives in all of America. She spent hours in quiet reflection and in thanksgiving and praise. She made some lists and reevaluated her priorities. She renewed her relationship with the Lord, reaffirming her belief that God had a plan and purpose for her life that included care for her mother but also included activities that did not directly relate to her caregiving.

When she returned home, Iris began to bounce back in small bounces. She first informed her two sisters that they needed to provide financial help so Mom could be placed in the Alzheimer's specialty hospital for at least one week a month, with the intent of increasing that time as her mother adjusted to the new environment and caregivers. The sisters willingly agreed.

Then Iris began to attend some classes at a nearby college to study subjects she had "always wanted to study." She made some new friends at the college and actually found the lectures, group projects, and course readings invigorating and mind expanding. She said, "I began to see new horizons, and I also saw how some of what I was reading might be applied in my care for my mother."

Exhausted from Striving Too Much

Carol and her husband, Brent, were exhausted from both caregiving and *trying*. For four years they had done everything they knew to do to prolong the life of their daughter Lindsey.

Lindsey had cystic fibrosis, and for a number of years the

breathing treatments and medications—coupled with the fervent, faith-filled prayers of countless friends and members of their church—did wonders. But when Lindsey turned seventeen, her health took a turn for the worse. Carol and Brent went into hyper mode. They took Lindsey to every specialist they heard about, often traveling hundreds of miles and taking off months at a time to try new courses of treatment. Nothing worked.

Finally Lindsey was put onto a transplant list for new lungs. Days and weeks and months passed. Carol and Brent prayed, they encouraged their daughter in every way they could, and they planned fun visits and special day outings. Then suddenly, or so it seemed, Lindsey slipped into a coma and died within a day. Carol and Brent were heartbroken.

"We had tried and tried and tried," Carol said. "We believed with our whole hearts that God would heal Lindsey. We exhausted all of our own physical, emotional, and financial resources. And in the end we had to accept the fact that God had allowed us to have seventeen years with one of the sweetest children on earth, but then He had called her to be with Him."

After the funeral, Carol and Brent hardly knew what to do with their time. They also didn't have good communication skills with each other—through the years, the bulk of their conversation had focused on Lindsey, not on their own ideas, dreams, or needs. They sought out a counselor who wisely encouraged them to go away, just the two of them, to a place where they had never gone with Lindsey and to become reacquainted as a couple. Think *breathe*!

While away, they spent time in prayer and reading the Bible, as their counselor had also advised. Carol said, "We recognized that we had anger at God and that we were carrying a huge load of disappointment that we had not received God's miracle in the way we *wanted* it to unfold. We began to rethink our own responses and to ask the Lord to heal us and to turn our hearts toward each other again. And He did! We came away from that time with new beliefs about how God might use us as a couple and as individuals."

Identify the Stress and Eliminate the Excess

An overbooked schedule.

A level of caring that goes beyond what is truly helpful.

A degree of striving that does not produce desired results.

Each of these phenomena in a person's life can produce tremendous stress, not only in an individual, but in a marriage or family. With the stress comes exhaustion.

There are lots of biological and physiological aspects to exhaustion. Most of them come down to the flee-or-fight mechanism that God has built into every person. When we are confronted with a crisis, or perceived crisis, we will take one of two approaches: we will seek to remove ourselves from the cause of our stress (flee), or we will rail against it and attempt to conquer it (fight). This is true whether the spider is a real spider or a clump of dust and hair on the floor that just *looks* like a spider. It is true whether the dark image on the wall is being made by a real bear just outside the cabin door or by a stump in the woods that has cast a shadow in the moonlight.

Stress is highly individualized. Much of it is related to how we *regard* a situation. To one person, a circumstance might feel like an adventure filled with possibility. To another, the same circumstance might feel like a ton of bricks. Stress is not the same for each person.

Stress is not the same for each person.

We each face the challenge of knowing our own limitations and perspectives. Learn to identify what you consider to be stressful, and then do your best to eliminate the *excess* from your life. It might be the elimination of something on your weekly or monthly calendar. It might be a membership or a committee obligation that you have volunteered to take on. It might be a business in which you have struggled for some time to get to the level of profitability you desire, to no avail. It might be something you thought you'd like to learn or try or be a part of, but are finding that you have neither the time nor energy to pursue it at the level you'd like.

Keep in mind that your schedule is always subject, to a great degree, to your choices, and that even if you say no to an activity or membership today, you may want to or be able to say yes to participating in the future.

A young woman in her late twenties told me that she had decided to take a year off from dating. She said, "I was spending long hours at work, and in my evenings I was trying to get more involved in a neighborhood church. I simply didn't have the time or energy to go out several nights a week. My friends thought I was crazy. But it was one of the sanest things I did in my midtwenties! I enjoyed some quiet evenings just reading at home, listening to soothing music, and letting myself listen in silence at times to see if there was something God wanted to say to me. I think you could say that those quiet evenings were *breathe* times for me. Those evenings certainly reinforced my relationship with the Lord and reaffirmed what I deeply believe. There was a freedom in me from *not* feeling that I needed to be in hot pursuit of a relationship. After a year I began to say yes to people who asked me out. I had a much clearer perspective on relationships at that point. I knew better who I was, and therefore I knew more about what I wanted out of a relationship. Dating had been stressful to me prior to my year off. Now it was pleasurable."

By the way, this woman did begin to date someone who became her husband about three years later.

In evaluating your stress level and what it might mean for you to make priority and scheduling adjustments in your life, I encourage you to do these two things:

Ask God for His Priorities

Ask the Lord to reveal to you His priorities for your life, and to show you which memberships and relationships are ones that He is authorizing for you. You should never feel that you must take on every assignment or become a part of every group that invites your presence or participation. Find out what God desires for you to do, and do *only* that.

Ask God for His Peace

Ask the Lord to impart to you His ongoing peace. Ask Him to help you leave plenty of "white space" in your schedule and in any given day so you can spend time with Him, and so you might move through your day without rushing. You will find that as you walk in *peace*, you will be able to accomplish even more, and to find life more enjoyable—even the chores and mundane responsibilities. You may also find that you are more open to new experiences and encounters if you aren't under an intense got-to-get-it-done agenda.

Trust God to Renew and Energize You

A Bible woman named Hannah knew a special brand of stress and exhaustion. She had tried for years to become pregnant. Her husband loved her dearly, and she knew that even though he had taken a second wife (which was legally and culturally acceptable in her day), she was the favorite wife. That did not make her life easier. The other wife ridiculed her for her inability to conceive a child. Hannah not only felt the sting of that criticism, but also had an ache in her life for a child.

At an annual festival meal, her circumstances became overwhelming to her. She dissolved into deep sobs and rushed from the feast table to the entrance of the tabernacle, the most holy place in her world. There she poured out her heart to the

Lord—and with such deep emotional travail that the priest accused her of being drunk. She assured him that she was sober but deeply sad. And at that, he pronounced to her that God would grant her prayers.

That day Hannah apparently let go of the tremendous buildup of stress that she had been harboring, and not long after that she conceived! She dedicated the son that she bore to the Lord's service. And she went on to have five more children—three sons and two daughters (1 Samuel 1:1–20; 2:21).

Be assured today that if you are exhausted and stressed out—God has an energized and renewed life ahead for you!

Separate Yourself from Your Burdens

Let me suggest several things to do as you separate yourself from your daily routine and life's burdens.

Trust God to Meet Your Needs

Ask the Lord very directly to meet your needs and deepest desires, and trust Him for His answers in His timing and according to His methods. Come to the Lord with a great sense of expectancy. Although you may feel broken, you are anticipating renewal and healing.

Ask God to Show You Where to Start

Ask the Lord to show you a specific time and place for your rejuvenation process to begin—a place where you can breathe and reaffirm what you believe. While the process of breathing emotionally and spiritually is highly individualized, a woman does not need to be alone or isolated to breathe. Sometimes being alone can be helpful, especially if you are dealing with a problem that you know will impact your future. Decisions are often best made in solitude—just you and the Lord. At other times it is very helpful to have close friends nearby, especially if they are also seeking a time with the Lord to breathe.

Seek God's Plans and Purposes

Be quick to humble yourself before the Lord and seek His plans and purposes. Once you have an understanding of what He is calling you to do, seek ways to lay aside all obligations and responsibilities that do not line up with His plan.

Pray for Refreshing Rest

Ask the Lord to help you experience deep rest and good sleep. If I have a busy day and collapse into bed without letting go of the day, the day can continue to fill my dreams and keep me from the rest and renewal that comes with deep sleep. I must "let go" before I "take on." That's true daily. It's also true for the larger issues of life.

Get Ready for Joy!

Anticipate an infusion of joy and purpose. Even as the Lord helps you to de-stress your life, He is likely to infuse you with new energy to take on the challenges that will truly delight your soul and bring you fulfillment. When that happens, you will find that you no longer feel the pain of the drain. The emptiness inside you will begin to fill with joy, and you will find yourself dreaming new dreams that send your heart soaring!

CHAPTER 4

Break Out of Your Limitations

Nobody can make you feel inferior without your consent.
—*Eleanor Roosevelt*

"I am *so* stuck."

That was Karen's appraisal of her circumstances. She put great emphasis on the word *so*.

When I didn't respond immediately, she added, "Like in quicksand."

Karen felt bound up in a set of limitations that she felt were holding her back from the pursuit of her dreams. Indeed, there were several things in Karen's life that many people would have considered to be debilitating or confining.

First, Karen had been born with a deformity in her hip sockets. She walked with a pronounced limp and was in a great deal of pain. She had never been able to run or skip or go on a ski trip. She said, "I'm grateful I can walk, but I sure wish I could walk faster and without pain."

Second, Karen was the daughter of first-generation immigrants to the United States. Her parents had moved to

America from Czechoslovakia in the late 1960s, when Karen was only a year old. Her name was actually Anna Karina but her parents had thought calling her Karen would make her assimilation into the American culture easier. She had grown up speaking Czech at home, in a neighborhood that also allowed her to learn Polish and Hungarian. "It was an Eastern European enclave," she said. "Nobody really fit in, and therefore everybody fit in—to a degree." Breaking out of an Eastern European mind-set had been a major challenge for her. She believed she had overcome her accent, but at times she realized she was sounding, in her terminology, "old world."

Third, Karen's parents were self-proclaimed atheists, but in Karen's view, "I think they believed there *might* be a God, so perhaps they were agnostics. I don't know. They would never discuss anything related to God with me—and especially after they knew I was a self-proclaimed Christian. The result was that I grew up knowing little to nothing about God or Christianity, and absolutely nothing about the Bible or church."

Karen had met a young Christian man while helping a neighbor do some home remodeling and repair work. "I was there to be a helpful friend who lived up the street, mostly keeping the workers in lemonade and sandwiches, and he was there on a mission project for his church. We talked easily and one thing led to the next, and almost before I knew it I was getting married. We attended his church, but for years I felt that I was 'behind' in the faith journey that everyone seemed to be on. I had so many things to learn, and even after I accepted Jesus as my Savior and began to grow spiritually, I felt inadequate around so many of the people in the church. Mostly I listened and tried to absorb what others said, but frankly, many parts of the Bible are still a mystery to me."

When I asked Karen how this might be a limiting factor in her life, she said, "In the situation I'm facing, I wish I knew more how to *defend* my faith and present it as an asset."

Fourth, Karen felt that she *could* have been successful in college and, in retrospect, *should* have done everything possible to *go* to college. She had taken a couple of courses at the community college and then entered the workforce. "I needed to support myself, so I worked hard and made my own way the best I could. I took time out when the children were born, and then when I went back to the workplace, a friend of my husband told me about a job in the lab where he works. It was work I could do and when I was given the opportunity, I worked hard and have now been there fifteen years."

Even so, Karen admitted that she frequently felt unqualified in doing her work for a biochemical lab. "I know the procedures I've been taught to do, and I understand the basics of what it is that we are trying to discover in many of the tests we are running, but I can't really explain *why* our work is important or how it has a practical application to more than a few thousand sick people."

Now Karen was facing a major challenge. Her daughter had given birth to a baby while living overseas, and she had returned home unmarried and with an eighteen-month-old son who had some health problems related to a drug habit her daughter had also acquired overseas. Karen wanted to gain custody of the child, but the biological father of the baby had surfaced and was also voicing a desire to have custody of the little boy. Her daughter, Sophia, was willing to enter a rehab hospital, was *unwilling* to release custody to the boy's father, and was further unwilling even to admit to him that the little boy was his son.

From Karen's perspective, Sophia was not at all emotionally or physically capable of caring for her son, and while Karen wasn't seeking to adopt her grandson, she was facing a very real possibility that this might be inevitable.

She said, "I talked to the people at Child Protective Services and they questioned my own physical ability to care for a toddler. The woman who interviewed me snorted when I told her about my husband and the church we attend. She said, 'It would be easier if you weren't religious fanatics.' She questioned how I could juggle work and the care of a little boy. She kept asking me to repeat words and even said at one point, 'Where *are* you from?' I also overheard her say to a coworker, 'I don't know why this woman thinks she can be a good mother to her grandson when her own daughter grew up to be a druggie.' *Everything* seems to be stacked against me."

I did my best to assure Karen of God's love, and I suggested she ask the Lord for very specific wisdom and guidance about the situations she was facing. She agreed to spend a little time breathing and believing.

Her circumstances, however, lingered in my mind and heart for some time.

I realized that I have met dozens of women in the last couple of years who feel imprisoned by circumstances in their lives. They feel limited and bound up, incapable of getting free to pursue the things that they believe God has for them to be and to do.

Some feel a racial barrier they can't seem to cross.

Others feel age discrimination. One woman said to me, "I like the senior-citizen discounts but I sure don't like being discounted because I'm a senior citizen!"

Others admit to feeling social ostracism. "I'm not part of the 'in' crowd," one woman lamented. "I didn't mind this at age sixteen nearly as much as I mind it at age forty-six!" Another woman said to me, "No matter how much I have succeeded in my work and family life, when I go back to my hometown I'm still the girl 'from the wrong side of the tracks.' I can't imagine that I would ever have any influence or even a good witness in the town where I grew up."

A few have told me that they are having difficulty finding a new church home after a move several hundred miles from their old home and church. A woman sighed deeply as she said to me, "We were part of a very closely knit small group in our former church, and every place now feels a bit foreign to us. We can't seem to break in or fit in, or maybe we can't seem to break *out* of feeling homesick for our old friends and old routines."

Prolonged sickness can dramatically change the way others think about us—and the way we think about ourselves. Several women have told me that they feel imprisoned by their own bodies. They have experienced diseases or injuries that have left them with "new normals." They don't like the restrictions they feel when it comes to mobility, flexibility, or stamina. And mostly they don't like the stigma of being "infirm" or a disease "victim." They admit to this stigma being in their own minds as much as in the mind of others.

Prolonged sickness can dramatically change the way others think about us—and the way we think about ourselves.

A few women told me how they have been struggling just to make ends meet financially—some have experienced a job loss or their husband has lost a job. A lack of financial resources is keeping them from giving or participating in projects or mission-trip opportunities they deeply desire to pursue.

In many cases, women have told me they feel hedged in by limitations—often with more than one type of limitation coming against them at a time. These are women who have dreams and who eagerly want to pursue them. But they feel their dreams sliding away as time goes by.

A Woman Who Lived as a Social Outcast

One of the wonderful miracles of Jesus involved a woman who truly was imprisoned by circumstances in her life. She doesn't have a name given to her, but we know a great deal about her.

This woman's story is told in several of the Gospels, and each Gospel writer seems to give specific details that, when put together, reveal a fairly dire circumstance that had her bound up with at least three different sets of limiting factors (Matthew 9:20–22; Mark 5:25–34; Luke 8:40–48).

She Was Sick in Her Body

We are told that this woman had been "subject to bleeding for twelve years" and that there wasn't anybody who could heal her. The King James Version calls it an "issue of blood," which implies that she was experiencing a nearly constant hemorrhage. This may have been the result of endometriosis or another similar ailment impacting her uterus. It may have been the result of uterine tumors. There is little doubt that her constant loss of blood over twelve years left her anemic and likely weak.

She Had Drained All Her Resources

We read in the Gospel of Mark, "She had suffered a great deal under the care of many doctors and had spent all she had, yet instead of getting better she grew worse" (Mark 5:26). Not only had this woman reached the end of her money, but she had suffered even more from the treatments that had been prescribed for her.

She Was a Social Outcast

The Law of Moses required that a woman who was hemorrhaging, or even experiencing normal menstruation, remain "apart" from others as long as she was bleeding. Women bleeding were considered unclean and were expected to keep their distance from others in the marketplace or on the streets of a village. If they did need to go out in public, they were to call out, "Unclean, unclean," if anybody came close to them. Those with a perpetual flow of blood were not allowed to participate in the feasts, festivals, and solemn assemblies associated with their faith. They were prohibited from coming to the synagogue, where they would have been in close proximity to other people.

Can you imagine the way this woman's self-esteem must have plummeted during the twelve years of her condition? She likely was starving for close friendship and fellowship, and for the warmth of a tender hug or even a comforting hand on her shoulder.

I have no doubt that any dreams or goals that this woman may have had for her life were *literally* drained from her.

Then the day came when she "heard about Jesus" (Mark 5:27). She decided that she would get to Jesus regardless of the custom that had her segregated from her society or the fact that she would need to break the religious law to get close to Him. She jostled her way through the crowd, coming up behind Jesus, likely crouching low to the ground to keep from being noticed. She finally got close enough to reach out and touch the edge of His garment.

This woman had predetermined that if she could just touch the end of Jesus' garment, it would be the same as touching Jesus. She had very good reason, it turns out, to think that.

What many don't know is that every Jewish man who kept the prayer times of the Jewish faith wore a prayer shawl almost as an undergarment between their tunic and outer cloak. This garment was hidden from view most of the time, but during prayer times was readily accessible for them to pull up over their heads for prayers.

The prayer shawls were edged in fringe, and the fringe for each person's shawl was knotted in a way that made it one of a kind. In fact, in the time of Jesus, the fringe from a man's prayer shawl could be pressed into clay or wax to leave an imprint that was equal to a signature in our day. A man's identity could be determined by the sequencing, size, and spacing of the knots on a fringed garment.

In the eyes of this bleeding woman, the fringe at the lower edge of Jesus' prayer shawl, which likely was visible just along the bottom edge of his cloak, represented the full identity of Jesus. And Jesus seemed to affirm this after she had run her fingers along this line of fringe. He stopped the crowd and asked, "Who touched my clothes?"

The disciples were dumbstruck. With so many people pressing in so closely, how could one person's touch be distinguished or have an impact? Jesus, however, had perceived that "power had gone out from him" (Mark 5:30).

He spotted the woman and gave these encouraging words: "Take heart, daughter," he said, "your faith has healed you" (Matthew 9:22).

The woman was healed instantly.

Keep in mind that more than her body was healed in that encounter with Jesus. With the hemorrhage stopped, she could be declared clean by the priests at the synagogue and restored fully to her family, friends, and community. This meant that she was free to begin to trade things in the market and create goods and sell them. In all likelihood, her finances would have begun to improve that day, especially since she no longer had a need for a medical budget.

A second miracle happened hot on the heels of this one.

The woman who was healed of the issue of blood had interrupted Jesus as He was walking to the home of a synagogue leader named Jairus. Jairus had come to Jesus asking Him to heal his daughter. Then, as they walked, word came that Jairus' little girl had died.

When Jesus arrived at Jairus' home, the people were already into their traditional grief wailing. When Jesus said, "Stop wailing. She is not dead but asleep!" they laughed at Him (Luke 8:52–53).

One of our recent Extraordinary Women conference speakers addressed the idea that when trouble strikes us, we often draw an invisible line around ourselves to keep from further assault and to keep from disappointment. In many cases, those who do this have prayed about something in the past and have been disappointed that God did not answer their prayers as they desired. Thus they made a decision to keep God out of their current problem.

I see these wailing women at Jairus' house as having drawn a line between what they were willing to believe Jesus *might* do and what they felt certain He would not or could not do.

Jesus, of course, took the little girl by the hand, commanded her to get up, and then helped her rise off her bed as He told her parents to give her something to eat.

Have you drawn a line about a particular circumstance, saying, "I cannot trust God to deal with *this*"? Choose to erase that line! Never underestimate God's ability to restore and renew *your* life, even to raising back a relationship, dream, or possibility in your life that you thought was long since over or dead!

We must be careful never to set limits when it comes to what God can and can't do or will and won't do. It is the devil's lie that God does not love us and won't help us. The devil rarely whispers into people's lives that God *can't*. Rather, he says, "God won't."

Have you drawn a line about a particular circumstance, saying, "I cannot trust God to deal with *this*"? Choose to erase that line!

Jesus, however, says repeatedly in God's Word, "I will." And then He adds, "Trust me to do what is the very best for you now and in eternity."

What an amazing display of God's healing power the people saw that day in the miracles of Jairus' daughter and the woman with the issue of blood. God was definitely saying, "I can and I will."

A Crippled Woman Healed by Jesus

Luke the physician also tells us about a woman who was severely crippled. This woman was stooped over to the point that she could not look up. She saw her feet and the ground, not the faces of her friends or the sky above. The Bible says:

> Jesus was teaching in one of the synagogues, and a woman was there who had been crippled by a spirit for eighteen years. She was bent over and could not straighten up at all. When Jesus saw her, he called her forward and said to her, "Woman, you are set free from your infirmity." Then he put his hands on her, and immediately she straightened up and praised God. (Luke 13:10–13)

A few verses later in this account we read these words of Jesus to those who criticized Him for healing this woman on the Sabbath:

> You hypocrites! Doesn't each of you on the Sabbath untie your ox or donkey from the stall and lead it out to give it water? Then should not this woman, a daughter of Abraham, whom Satan has kept bound for eighteen long years, be set free on the Sabbath day from what bound her? (Luke 13:15–16)

These statements from Jesus let us know that this woman's condition was not osteoporosis or anything related to curvature of the spine. She was held in a crippled condition by emotional and spiritual forces that were attributed by Jesus to Satan.

The Bible speaks about several tricks of the enemy of our soul, among them demonic possession (a total takeover of a person's psyche and behavior), demonic oppression (an inhibiting and burdensome weight placed upon a person's inner being), and depression (a psychological "dimming of the soul" that is usually accompanied by discouragement and loss of hope). This woman seems to have been the victim of oppression. The physical bowing of her back—her stooped-over condition—reflected the stooped-over state of her inner soul.

She willingly went to the synagogue . . . but she remained bent over. In other words, the rituals associated with her faith did not have any impact on her spiritual state, her outlook, her flexibility, or on many of the functions that would have allowed her to be a fully contributing family or community member. A person who is stooped over is inflexible, likely in perpetual pain or discomfort, and is incapable of doing many physical chores.

Because Jesus referred to Satan having kept her bound, we can also assume that this woman's condition came upon her because of something spiritual that happened to her. She may very well have sinned in a way that was so troublesome and so severe that she could no longer "hold her head up in society." The humility of her confession became paralyzing and permanent.

Even if she personally had not sinned, she may have been the victim of shaming—which is the state that occurs when others accuse a person of wrongdoing or wrongful association to the point that the person truly believes she is a "bad person" even if she has not personally committed a sin.

There are many women who find themselves in a spiritually stooped-over condition. They may have received God's forgiveness, but they have never forgiven themselves for a mistake they made or a genuine sin they committed. They may not have stood up to shame and declared within themselves, "I am forgiven and I am beloved by God." They hang their heads emotionally and spiritually—even if they do not hang their heads physically. They feel deeply unworthy of God's love or the love of others.

There are also women who feel a severe lack of value because of the abusive opinions of others, often first heard in their childhood or for prolonged periods of their life. They have been told they are worth nothing, can do nothing, know nothing, and will never amount to anything. Such a constant barrage of insults and criticism can cause a person to develop extremely low self-worth. A woman who has been verbally abused in these ways may have never heard about God's love and approval—or if she has heard the message of God's love, she has refused to believe it.

Such women tend to be bowed over, often to the point where they are incapable of straightening themselves.

Before we talk about God's remedies, let me share with you one more example of a woman bound up in a prison of circumstantial limitations.

A Woman Who Received No Justice

Jesus told a parable about a woman who may as well have been in a prison. She was not free to pursue her dreams or fulfill her potential because of the way another person had treated her. Here is the story Jesus told:

> In a certain town there was a judge who neither feared God nor cared what people thought. And there was a widow in that town who kept coming to him with the plea, "Grant me justice against my adversary."
>
> For some time he refused. But finally he said to himself, "Even though I don't fear God or care what people think, yet because this widow keeps bothering me, I will see that she gets justice, so that she won't eventually come and attack me!" . . .
>
> Listen to what the unjust judge says. And will not God bring about justice for his chosen ones, who cry out to him day and night? Will he keep putting them off? I tell you, he will see that they get justice, and quickly. (Luke 18:2–8)

Because this woman is described as a widow, we can assume that her "adversary" may very well have been the person who caused the death of her husband. Or her adversary may have been someone who was keeping her from an inheritance or from ownership of the property of her deceased husband. She was being denied what was rightfully hers. Either way, she wanted justice and she kept going to the judge.

Jesus used this story to teach about prayer and the importance of prayer in our receiving justice for anything that the enemy of our souls has taken from us. Jesus taught that the devil is a thief and a liar, and He said about the devil, "The thief comes only to steal and kill and destroy; I have come that they may have life, and have it to the full" (John 10:10).

Countless women today spend their days in the courts of our nation because a loved one has been killed or maimed. They are seeking justice.

Many others are involved in lawsuits and adversarial relationships because of what others owe them financially or because of what has been stolen from them.

Still others are in personal campaigns to bring attention to conditions or instances in which they have been wrongfully defamed, displaced, or had their reputations damaged by what others have said or done.

Those who are in these circumstances are living in a type of prison that totally occupies their minds, hearts, and time. Their quest for justice often robs them of resources and finances. Many become disillusioned and, at times, experience a serious challenge to their faith.

How Are We to Break Free?

Consider how Jesus related to these three women, and what He offered to them and to us as the *way* in which we are to break out of the inner prisons that keep us from pursuing the fulfillment of our hopes and dreams:

- Jesus calls upon us to use our *faith*. Jesus commended the woman with the issue of blood for her faith, and He went so far as to say it was her faith that led her to wholeness.

- Jesus calls upon us to *take heart*. Jesus noted the fear registered in the eyes and demeanor of the woman who had touched the edge of his garment. He told her to be encouraged, to "take heart!"

- Jesus calls upon us to *seek His delivering power*. We cannot deliver ourselves. The woman who was crippled could *not* straighten herself. But, to her great credit, she had gone to a place where the faithful gathered. It was in a place where faith was expected to function that she truly did experience the function of faith!

- Jesus calls upon us to *persist in prayer*. The widow seeking justice was commended by Jesus in His parable for her relentless prayer. She did not stop asking God to meet her need and resolve her problem, and to give her what was rightfully hers.

Let me bring this to a practical conclusion.

Breathe!

When you set yourself apart to breathe, that space or place to which you retreat should never be perceived as a prison. You may be shutting out the world or withdrawing from your life for a brief period, but refuse to see this as a confining cage or cave. Instead see it as a place of refuge where you can curl up in the everlasting arms of the Lord and listen to His heartbeat and hear His tender whispers of mercy and love.

Choose to establish your retreat as a place to rekindle your faith, to pray, and to be encouraged in the Lord.

The Bible tells us that when David was most discouraged, He "found strength in the LORD his God" (1 Samuel 30:6). How did David do this? The Bible doesn't give us specific details but I am convinced that David went apart to spend some concerted time strumming his lyre and singing praises to the Lord. Praise was the key to David's experiencing the renewal of his spirit. Praise was the key to his restoration of joy.

As a vital part of your breathing, breathe in the presence of the Lord and exhale your praise to God.

Believe!

If you see your circumstances as confining and limiting, ask God to break down the walls of the prison that has encapsulated your soul.

Declare the truth:

- My negative circumstances are *not* omnipotent or omnipresent. God *is* more powerful than my circumstances. God not only will outlast my problem, but He will subdue my problem so that it is of no importance and not worth remembering!

- My problem is *not* higher than God. No! God is truly greater than my problem. The Bible tells me that every knee shall bow to the Lord (Philippians 2:10). That means anything that is seeking to destroy me—in my body, my mind, my emotions, my marriage, my finances, my reputation, my friendships, *anything* that has taken on the role of an enemy—*must* bow to the Lord. He rules and reigns in my life, not my problem.

- No enemy can withstand the Lord. God *will* bring something good out of this situation. He will lift my feet out of the miry clay and set me on the path of righteousness so I might fulfill His plans and purposes for me. He will defeat my adversaries and give me divine justice!

Prepare to *Bounce Back!*

As you prepare to bounce back, you may want to think of this as bouncing *over* all the limitations or barriers that seem to have you hedged in.

I made a little list on one occasion of the ways in which we overcome barriers that seem to press in on us from all sides. Consider these phrases:

- *leap over*
- *pole vault outta here*
- *climb over*
- *soar over*
- *break out*
- *move beyond*

In other words, get free! Ask the Lord to give you bounce-back energy and strength. Ask Him to show you what to say, what to do, and most important, where to focus your prayers and faith.

Ask Him to send you those who can pray for and with you, encourage you, and walk with you into a newness of life.

What Happened to Karen?

At the outset of this chapter, I told you about Karen.

Karen went on a several-day retreat to seek the Lord's presence. Her husband went with her, and *together* they took time to breathe in the love and mercy and tenderness of the Lord. They began to talk about God's highest and best—as it related to their personal lives and their marriage, as it related to their daughter, and as it related to their grandson. They made a list of Bible verses that encapsulated what they believed about God's desire for their young grandchild to be protected, provided for, and nurtured. They did the same for God's desire to heal and restore their daughter. And they asked God for specific wisdom about what they should do.

Karen said, "One passage kept coming to our minds again and again: 'If any of you lacks wisdom, you should ask God, who gives generously to all without finding fault, and it will be given to you. But when you ask, you must believe and not doubt, because the one who doubts is like a wave of the sea, blown and tossed by the wind'" (James 1:5–6).

Karen went on to say, "We began to feel very strongly that we should ask God to give us the guardianship of our grandson, but to do it in His way, not our way."

A month later their daughter voluntarily entered a rehab hospital. She was there for six weeks. When she came out of the hospital, she went to her parents, asked for their forgiveness, told them that she had accepted Jesus as her Savior while in the hospital, and asked them to adopt her son!

Karen said, "We had no idea that we could adopt in that manner, without anybody from the Child Protective Services agency involved. We had been taking care of our grandson the entire time our daughter was in the hospital. We agreed to the adoption and also agreed that she could remain in her son's life as 'Auntie Sophia' as long as she remained clean and sober."

Karen also said, "The biological father disappeared. He had been insistently badgering Sophia, but then one day he wrote her a little note and said, 'I'm going home. Do what you want.' He never came calling again."

It is now five years later. We know that God did things *His* way, in *His* timing, and by *His* methods.

Karen also told me this: "My husband and I go away once a year for a few days. We go to breathe and to take stock of where we are in our marriage, in our personal goals, and in our parenting of our grandson. We spend much of our days talking about the goodness of the Lord and reminding ourselves of the ways in which God has enabled us to overcome so much and to receive such wonderful miracles from His hand. And we always find ourselves with renewed energy and strength to bounce back into our daily responsibilities. I am convinced— your idea of *breathe, believe,* and *bounce back* is not a one-time deal. It should be a once-a-year appointment with the Lord."

What can I add except *yes*!

CHAPTER 5

Say No to Despair

It is impossible for that man to despair who
remembers that his Helper is omnipotent.
—*Jeremy Taylor*

Carissa was one of those people who seemed to be the "forever cheerleader." I'm not talking about a cheerleader of the high-school pep squad variety. I'm talking about a person who was bright and sunny in personality, forever quick to give a word of personal encouragement or a "Way to go!" word of approval and applause.

Then the day came when she collapsed emotionally. Before her friends even realized the full extent of what was happening, Carissa ended up in a psychiatric hospital with severe depression.

Nobody saw it coming. Nobody saw a reason for her rapid emotional decline. There appeared to be no triggering event—no specific cause or crisis—that resulted in her slide toward despair.

Many who knew her could not fathom how a strong believer in Christ Jesus might suddenly feel so bereft or be so willing to curl up in her bed or begin to entertain a desire to die.

Including Carissa. *She* could not understand the darkness that enveloped her and seemed to demand her submission to it. She recalls saying to a friend, "My psyche is broken and I don't know why."

In truth, depression is a factor in the lives of millions of women today—often those we regard as least likely to become depressed. And yes, Christians with strong faith *can* become depressed! The statistics tell us women are twice as likely as men to suffer from depression. About one in five women can expect to suffer from clinical depression at some point in their lives.

We need to recognize at the outset of our consideration of depression that there are many types of depression and many causes for depression. Every person's situation is slightly different, and therefore there are no universal remedies.

Some depression is rooted in a physical ailment or an imbalance in the biological systems of the body or brain. Before any form of therapeutic treatment can be prescribed by a psychologist or psychiatrist, a full battery of physical tests is often run. Hormones can run amuck, chemicals in the brain can become unbalanced, physiological processes can become skewed, endocrine secretions can become depleted, nerves can cease to function normally—the body has *countless* ways of manifesting disarray and brokenness.

For a woman who is depressed, an important preliminary step to *breathing* is likely to be a visit to a physician for a complete physical workup. Many emotional conditions cannot be fully addressed and overcome if a chemical imbalance, stubborn infection, or severe nutritional deficiency is present.

Some depression is brought upon by trauma—one or more sudden and overwhelming events might send a person tumbling emotionally. A woman who is hit with sudden and extreme loss can become disoriented and have feelings of shock. It might be the death of a loved one or the diagnosis of a life-threatening disease or the loss of all one's possessions in a fire, flood, or tornado. A life that seemed to be proceeding normally can spin out of control.

Some depression builds up slowly, it seems. Years of unresolved guilt or shame, undiagnosed and untreated emotional problems, or dysfunctional, abusive behavior can build to a tipping point of inner pain.

You—and a godly therapist—have the responsibility for getting to the core of your depression. Confront your depressed feelings—sooner rather than later! If you are depressed even mildly today, I encourage you to run, not walk, to a godly counselor who can help you turn things around, someone whose wisdom and input flows from the Wonderful Counselor into your heart and life. A good place to begin is AACC.net (the website of the American Association of Christian Counselors) and check out their Find a Counselor link.

What we can do in a book like this, however, is deal with two broad truths.

First, depression in all its forms can cause a woman to have diminished hope, and in that state begin to feel her dreams are sliding away from her. Depression can cause inner pain and feelings of growing emptiness and futility.

Depression is something we must not deny. It is not something we should ever take lightly. Depression does not further our growth, expand our energy, or propel us to new heights of service to others. The opposites occur: depression stifles our growth, depletes our energy, and drags us down to the point where we often cannot see any needs beyond those staring back at us in our own mirror.

Second, the prevailing evidence of God's Word reveals that God desires for us to live in a state of joy, peace, and purpose. He wants us to walk in the abiding truth of His Word and be filled with the comfort of His presence. Depression is not part of God's desire for any person; His desire is to heal us and make us whole.

Enemy Tactics: Lies and Fears

There is an enemy of your soul—Satan, who does *not* want you to bounce back. He will move against you with countless lies in an attempt to get you to give up, to silence your voice.

Depression is often an elixir of the devil's lies and fears, shaken together in a subtle disguise to deceive us.

Jesus called the enemy of our souls "the father of lies" (John 8:44). The devil is totally incapable of telling the whole truth about anything. He is adept, instead, at innuendo, half-truths, and a general glossing over of reality. He has a long track record of subtle deceit.

The devil is also an instigator of fears—the debilitating, crippling kind. Depression is often an elixir of the devil's lies and fears, shaken together in a subtle disguise to deceive us.

Carissa did emerge from her depression. It took months of hospitalization and still more months of counseling and medications. Several years after this dark period in her life, she identified some of the fears and lies that had gripped her. She said: "I started imagining things that *could* be wrong and that *might* happen. My husband traveled in his business a great deal of time and I found myself thinking, *He doesn't love me or he'd find a way to stay home more. He probably has a woman in each of the major cities where he does business. He'll abandon me one day.* I had no evidence to support any of these ideas, but the reality of my life—alone much of the time—didn't match up with the romance novels I was reading or the romantic movies I was watching.

"Of course when I began to think about what seemed like an eventual abandonment by my husband, I also began to panic at all I would lose *besides* my husband. I thought, *I'll lose my home. I'll no longer have the luxury of working just half time for the joy of working—I'll need to work full time and overtime just to feed myself and my two cats! I'll lose all sense of personal security and provision.* The truth, of course, was that my husband had not abandoned me.

"Then I began to think, *What if my husband died in a plane crash with all his traveling around the world? Where would I turn? What don't I know that I should know? Would I ever find someone to love and marry if he did leave me for another woman or leave me in death?* The more I let these thoughts and fears fill me, the more I fueled whatever else was a factor in my depression!

"And then I began to think about my daughter: *She is going to move away to go to college and leave me all alone, and then she'll get married and have a child that I never get to see. She already doesn't want to go to church, and she just may slide away completely from the Lord, and how would I ever bear the pain of knowing that my child was rebelling against God?* The truth was that after she graduated from college and was hired by a good company, my daughter moved out of our home to an apartment close to her place of employment, about twenty miles away.

"The more my fears built up, the more I felt guilty for feeling fearful. I began to think, *What kind of Christian am I? I can't trust God with the most basic relationships in my life. How can I be a true witness to others of God's love if I don't seem to believe that He loves me enough to provide for me and to protect my husband and daughter? I am a failure in my faith!* The truth was I was spending too much time alone thinking about myself and not enough time developing close friends who could encourage me in the Lord.

"At the same time I was developing these fears, people in my church had started to see me as a leader, and the more they did so, the less they seemed to want to get together for coffee and conversation as equals in friendship. I didn't realize that I was becoming more isolated until I truly was isolated. If I had been talking about some of these things openly and candidly with mature Christian friends, I think they might have advised me to get my head *out* of the romance novels and turn my attention *away* from the soap operas and stay busy helping people in interdependent ways."

The main lies and fears that seemed to develop in Carissa and become factors related to her depression are the same ones I see in several Bible women who were key players in the lives of the prophets Elijah and Elisha. The fears and lies embodied by these women are ones that strike many women, perhaps *all* women, to at least some degree at some point in their lives. Now, not all women who are associated or impacted by them develop depression—but these lies and fears *can* put a woman on a downward spiral toward deep despair. We need to be aware of the tricks of the enemy so we can take action early rather than later.

Lies and fears *do* assail our hopes and dreams. They *do* drain us emotionally!

The Fear of Personal Destruction

Elijah was a powerful leader in his day—a prophet of God consulted by kings and queens, a man who experienced miracles and was used by God to bring great healing and deliverance to many in ancient Israel. As such, he was also despised by those who did *not* want the God of Israel directing their lives. One of those who hated Elijah with a passion was a wicked queen named Jezebel.

Jezebel was not an Israelite—she had been chosen as a wife by Ahab, a king of Israel who sought to make a political alliance with the king of Sidon, who ruled the territory north of Ahab. Jezebel was the daughter of Ethbaal, the king of the Sidonians, and she was a woman who had been raised to worship the false gods Baal and Asherah. She influenced Ahab to turn away from Jehovah God and build altars and shrines to her gods, and to employ more than eight hundred prophets of Baal and Asherah.

The Bible tells us that Elijah was ordered by God to confront these men who led the worship of false gods. A powerful showdown took place on Mount Carmel and it was one of the most dramatic days in the history of ancient Israel. An altar was built and an agreement was struck: the god who answered by fire—consuming the sacrifice offered—was God.

The Baal and Asherah prophets danced and chanted before their altar and sacrifice all day, cutting themselves as part of their ritual. Nothing happened. Elijah then stepped up at the time of the Jewish evening sacrifice, thoroughly doused his sacrifice and altar with water, and even filled a moat around the altar with water. He called upon God, and immediately fire came out of heaven and consumed the sacrifice. He was a clear winner in this battle between evil and good.

Before the end of that day, hundreds of prophets of Baal and Asherah had been slain and a longstanding drought was declared to be over. When Jezebel heard what Elijah had done to "her" priests, she sent word to Elijah: "May the gods deal with me, be it ever so severely, if by this time tomorrow I do not make your life like that of one of [these dead prophets]" (1 Kings 19:2). The Bible tells us that "Elijah was afraid and ran for his life" (1 Kings 19:3). He escaped by himself to Mount Horeb, and went into a cave there. (See 1 Kings 18:16–19:3 for the complete story.)

The Lord used a mighty wind, an earthquake, and a manifestation of fire to get Elijah's attention. And when Elijah was finally ready to listen—perhaps ready to listen because he had laid aside his fears—he heard the voice of the Lord as a "still small voice." God asked, "What are you doing here, Elijah?" (1 Kings 19:12–13).

It seems that many women who are depressed become ensnared in questioning along the lines of, "Why is this happening? Why isn't God helping me? Why am I so down?" The better question to ask may be, "What am I going to do about this? How am I going to move forward?"

Only so much can be gained by looking back and analyzing the past. There is much more to be gained by looking at resources presently available and turning one's attention to the future. Even if a person doesn't have the physical, emotional, or mental energy to dream new dreams or set new goals, a person *can* begin to believe God does have a future plan and purpose. A person can begin to believe that healing can occur and that the future *can* be bright again.

Elijah was still in a state of dejection, however, as he replied, "I have been very zealous for the LORD God Almighty. The Israelites have rejected your covenant, torn down your altars, and put your prophets to death with the sword. I am the only one left, and now they are trying to kill me too" (1 Kings 19:14).

You can almost hear the self-pity, depression, and weariness in his voice, can't you?

I want you to see clearly that this cave on Mount Horeb was *not* a place of retreat where Elijah went so he might breathe. It was a place of escape where he sought to hide out and perhaps die.

When we go apart for a time of recovery, we must make certain that we are *expecting* to emerge from that place renewed, stronger, and with new insights and energy.

The second thing I encourage you to recognize is that even the most spiritually powerful man in all of ancient Israel at that time was *afraid*. Every person can become afraid—no person is immune from an attack of fear. You might even say he had a panic attack.

Do you have an enemy today—perhaps someone who is determined to persecute you and others who believe the way you do about God? Are you subject to ongoing, persistent, and intense criticism or ridicule? Are you being threatened— perhaps not with your life but with the loss of a job, the torching of your church, an attack against your family, or some other force of evil that can destroy your integrity, reputation, and ability to provide for and protect yourself and those you love? If so, you are a candidate for the kind of depression that Elijah no doubt felt in the cave of Horeb.

Jezebel was the queen . . . but on the other hand, she was just one person. Elijah had confronted hundreds of false prophets and defeated them. Even so, he knew that Jezebel had ordered the killing of *most* of the Israelite prophets. Her wishes had become Ahab's command, and dastardly deeds had been done. Elijah had good reason to fear, but it was fear coupled with the lie, "You're next," that drove Elijah into isolation and what he felt certain would be a place of starvation and death.

The lesson for us? The enemy of our soul often uses *people* to put in place the factors related to our depressed feelings.

A Negative Spiral of Fears and Lies

Depression very often follows a sequence of feelings, fears, and lies. We become frustrated that things are not going our way, and we start to fear that they might never go our way, and the lie seeps in: "Things *should* be going your way but apparently God has abandoned you and is now punishing you for something."

The truth is that God has never promised us that life is going to flow in perfection. He has promised that He will walk through life's dark periods with us. And furthermore, the truth is that God does not seek to destroy His faithful followers—He may chastise us for disobedience, but His purpose is always to get us back on the track of obedience. God does not abandon His people.

If we allow frustration to continue, we can become discouraged. Discouragement generally comes with a sense of weariness—we are trying and trying, and nothing is going right.

We start to fear that we will never succeed, and we begin to swallow the lie that God no longer hears our prayers or is on our side.

If we continue in discouragement, the discouragement often grows deeper and we become disillusioned with all of life. We see wickedness and darkness in every direction we turn, and we begin to fear that we will be swallowed up by evil. We believe the lie that God no longer has any concern for us or that He is incapable of helping us.

Are you struggling with unresolved frustration, discouragement, disillusionment, or depression? Choose to confront the downward spiral!

And if this deep discouragement continues, we can readily find ourselves depressed. If we don't check the depression and get help for it, we can move into despair, and if that continues, death may result.

Are you struggling with unresolved frustration, discouragement, disillusionment, or depression? Choose to confront the downward spiral!

A Positive Upward Spiral

The good news is that there is an *upward* sequence that is more powerful than the downward spiral to depression.

First, we can defeat frustration by reminding ourselves daily that God loves us, and He has promised to turn *all* things to our good in His timing and by His methods. We *can* remain faithful even if life's circumstances are stacking up against us. We must bring these thoughts to our own minds, and the best way I know is to memorize verses of Scripture and recite them to ourselves.

For most of us, this is also a challenge to turn on the praise music in our homes and cars, and turn off the news and the programs that seem to project very little beyond violence and sexual lust.

Second, we can adopt a discipline of voicing our gratitude and praise to God. Give thanks to God for what He has done, is doing, and has promised to do—which is what He *will* do. Words of praise are for the unchanging attributes of God—they remind us of who God is and always will be.

Words of thanksgiving build our confidence that God has always taken care of us.

Words of praise build our faith that God is in control and in His all-powerful, all-wise, ever-present, and all-loving nature, He will show us mercy.

Praise is deeply rooted in an awareness that God is *near*— He is present with us.

The apostle Paul admonished the Philippians to "Rejoice in the Lord always. I will say it again: Rejoice! Let your gentleness be evident to all. The Lord is near" (Philippians 4:4–5). The key to rejoicing lies in *knowing* deep inside that the Lord is near.

When you are on a retreat to breathe, perhaps the foremost thing you can do to prepare yourself for bouncing back is to reaffirm God's love and near presence. Read the Scriptures aloud. Write out passages that speak strongly to you and keep them in a journal or on note cards to which you can refer often.

And then immerse yourself as you reaffirm what you believe by spending a length of time in thanksgiving and praise. Recount things both little and big that God has done for you, given to you, or enabled you to do. Nothing is too grand or too ordinary for thanks! You can never run out of things for which to thank God.

Force yourself to move beyond the standard attributes that you may have used in your praise of the Lord. Think of as many facets of His wonderful nature as possible!

Don't be dismayed if an hour or two of thanks and praise doesn't restore you to a *vast* amount of joy or peace. Stay at it! Spend time the next day in more thanks and praise. Begin to make it a habit of your life. And as you offer a "sacrifice" of thanks and praise—giving to the Lord your time, energy, and focus—ask the Lord to give you a growing confidence and faith that He is acutely aware of you and your situation and that He has a plan for your healing from depression.

The Lord spoke to Elijah, reminding him that He was *not* alone as Elijah had thought. There were other prophets elsewhere in the land who were alive and serving the Lord. In fact, the Lord revealed to him that there were seven thousand prophets who were faithful to the God of Israel!

The Lord also sent Elijah to anoint a new king and to seek out Elisha as his successor. Elijah emerged from Horeb with purpose and with a new focus for his life. If you are depressed today, begin to believe that God most definitely has a bounce-back future for you!

The Fear of Dying in a Catastrophe

Elijah's experience with Jezebel came after a multiyear drought that God had used to bring Israel to repentance. Shortly after the drought began, the Lord had led Elijah to move east of the Jordan River to a place near the Kerith Ravine. There, Elijah was fed by ravens that brought him morsels of bread and meat every morning and again in the evening. He drank from the brook. Since the king's palace was likely the only place with ongoing food and scraps of meat and bread, these ravens were perhaps bringing Elijah the leftovers from Ahab's dwelling!

Then when the ravens stopped coming and the brook dried up, Elijah was sent by the Lord to the little town of Zarephath, where the Lord said, "I have commanded a widow in that place to supply you with food."

When Elijah arrived, he found a woman gathering sticks by the town gate and he asked her for a drink and a piece of bread. She replied that she didn't have any bread, only a little meal and a little oil. She expressed her intent to make a small meal for herself and her son, and she also indicated to him that she fully expected this to be their last meal before they died of starvation!

We do not read in the Bible that this woman was depressed, but how could she have been anything else? She was the victim of a massive drought from which there was no escape and no relief. She was anticipating the death of herself and her son, and likely had only one hope: that her son would die before she did so he would be spared the agony of seeing his mother die. She made no proclamation of faith or hope to Elijah. She was apparently bound with fear as well as discouragement because Elijah's words back to her were, "Don't be afraid!"

Elijah commanded this woman to make a little cake from the bread and oil and to give it to him and then make a second little cake for herself and her son. He gave her these prophetic words of hope: "This is what the LORD, the God of Israel, says, 'The jar of flour will not be used up and the jug of oil will not run dry until the day the LORD sends rain on the land'" (1 Kings 17:14).

She did as Elijah commanded, and things turned out exactly as he had prophesied. The Bible tells us, "There was food every day for Elijah and for the woman and her family. For the jar of flour was not used up and the jug of oil did not run dry" (1 Kings 17:15–16). This woman may very well have experienced three full years of provision from an almost empty supply of flour and oil. (See 1 Kings 17:1–16 for the complete story.)

For many people, financial problems and debt are a major source of depression. They are living on the edge of losing their homes, losing their valued possessions, and perhaps becoming unemployed. Few things are as debilitating as not having enough to properly care for one's children. This woman perhaps had to fight back fears every day. She never did experience an overflowing amount of oil or flour—only enough for that day.

I believe this woman was in a position to *need* an ongoing flow of affirmation about what she believed. She needed to say often, "God has been faithful. He was faithful yesterday. I can trust Him to be faithful to the prophet's words today. I can hope for tomorrow."

Those are major affirmation statements to keep in mind if depression settles on a person's mind and emotions. God is faithful. As a friend of mine says, "I checked this morning and God has not moved one micromillimeter off His throne!" God is still in control of His universe and He has ways of meeting our needs and renewing us that we can't even imagine!

**Are your eyes on the world and today's bad news,
or on God's good news?**

If we allow ourselves to get our eyes on the world as a whole—with all of its upheaval, lack of food, economic turmoil, wars and rumors of wars, and rampant disease and threats of major viral outbreaks—we can easily fall into fear and the trap of thinking, *All of this can't help but overwhelm and overtake me.* The opposite way of thinking is the way of faith: *God is in control. God is faithful. I will trust Him. I can't do anything about the world as a whole, but I can take charge of my own words and declare, "I will trust God!"*

Are your eyes on the world and today's bad news, or on God's good news?

The Fear of Losing Everything of Value

Elisha, the great prophet who was trained by Elijah and who succeeded Elijah, also knew something about multiplied oil.

Elisha was in charge of a "school" for training prophets. One day a person associated with that school died. His widow came to Elisha and said, "Your servant my husband is dead, and you know that he revered the LORD. But now his creditor is coming to take my two boys as his slaves" (2 Kings 4:1).

Can you hear the frantic edge to this woman's voice? She is on the verge of losing everything. She has no income. Her husband died leaving a significant amount of debt for her to deal with. According to an acceptable custom of that time, the man who had loaned money to her deceased husband could claim her sons as his slaves to "work off" the debt. This idea, of course, would leave her further bereft and without the boys to help her with the daily support *she* needed.

She was facing a mountain of problems and sorrow and was on the verge of becoming *totally* destitute.

This woman was not the victim of a national calamity, as was the widow in Zarephath. She was nonetheless a victim of a very personal tragedy. She saw no way out. And that is a prime environment for depression to take hold. When a person sees nothing good in her future, she can't help but feel that someone is turning out the lights all around her.

Elisha asked her, "What do you have in your house?" She replied, "Your servant has nothing there at all," and then she added "except a little oil."

A depressed person very often feels that she has no talents, no strength, no energy, no value, no purpose—in sum, *nothing at all*. But in truth, every person has *something*. It may be just enough energy to get out of bed and wash your face. It may be just enough strength to boil an egg for breakfast. It may be just enough ability to call for a friend to come over to help.

Elisha immediately said, "Go around and ask all your neighbors for empty jars. Don't ask for just a few. Then go inside and shut the door behind you and your sons. Pour oil into all the jars, and as each is filled, put it to one side" (2 Kings 4:3–4).

She did this: her sons gathered jars, and she kept pouring . . . and pouring . . . and pouring. When all the available jars were full and her sons reported that they couldn't find another jar to bring to her, she told the man of God the status of things. Elisha said, "Go, sell the oil and pay your debts. You and your sons can live on what is left" (2 Kings 4:7).

There was enough money to be made from that oil for her to live and not die, and for her sons to remain with her and not enter servitude. It was a double bounce-back miracle!

The work that occurred in this story happened in private. In a way, her closing the door to the outside world was a small form of retreat in which she could focus only on the immediate and necessary tasks of a given day—in her case, the task of pouring oil from one container into other containers. (See 2 Kings 4:1–7 for the complete story.)

When you go away to breathe, and especially if you are depressed, you need to focus on your daily routine. Keep doing what you can do! Keep doing those things that you normally have done. Keep doing the basics that keep you fed and bathed and dressed. Maintain a schedule.

Don't let yourself get too tired. Don't let yourself get too hungry. Keep people around you. And stay active to the level that you can be productive at something.

Never let yourself feel too much *hunger* or too much *anger*; never let yourself become too *lonely* or too *tired*. In other words: H-A-L-T!

Never let yourself feel too much *hunger* or too much *anger*; never let yourself become too *lonely* or too *tired*. In other words: H-A-L-T!

There is no benefit to a depressed person curling up in a fetal position in her bed and hoping things will get better. Stay active to the degree you can be active!

Many people find it helpful to do something *physical* when they are depressed. They may be able to do a little handwork or woodwork. They may be able to do a little gardening. I know one woman who put together a couple of birdhouse kits and then painted them and sold them. She hadn't counted on starting a business. She was only doing something to amuse herself and to have something to show for her time. She told her friends later that nails and paint were the best medicine she took for her depression.

In addition to making birdhouses, she took on a hobby of making birdfeeders and of feeding birds that flew into her backyard. Feeding the birds and keeping a small birdbath filled with water gave her a good reason to get up on dark, wintry mornings. She looked forward to watching the birds come and go, and eventually she began to use the paints for the birdhouses to paint small scenes of her backyard birds. Yes, the birdfeeders and her paintings became two more streams of income.

These outlets for her creativity put her in touch with new friends. She began to teach little Bible studies about God's care of His creation and other lessons she had learned from her work. She later said, "I finally got to the place where I didn't have time to be depressed. I had too much to do!"

So did the woman filling every container she could find with oil that was replenished by the Lord.

God has *something* that you can do and are supposed to do. Following His directives will be an act of faith on your part, and it will be a key to bouncing back.

The Fears Associated with Our Children

Elisha had a profound experience with another woman described simply as "The Shunammite" (2 Kings 4:8–37).

One day as Elisha passed through the city of Shunem, he was invited by a woman who lived there to have a meal in her home. Thereafter, when Elisha went to Shunem he stopped at her house, usually with his servant Gehazi at his side. This woman suggested to her husband that they add a room to their home to show ongoing hospitality to Elisha and his servant, and her husband agreed.

Elisha wanted to do something to express his thanks

for her kindness and he sought a way to bring a blessing to her. He finally said to her, "About this time next year, you will hold a son in your arms." This woman's husband was old and she had no hopes of bearing a child, so she replied, "No, my lord! . . . Please, man of God, don't mislead your servant!" (2 Kings 4:16).

Those who work with depressed people find that those who are depressed have very little ability to receive compliments, or even words intended to encourage them. They simply don't feel worthy of any good thing—it is part of their depression that they cannot receive expressions of love and value. Recognize that tendency in yourself if you are depressed. Also recognize that tendency if you are living with or attempting to help someone who is depressed.

We must not promise ourselves too much. But we *can* voice the promise of God's Word to our own selves when we are depressed or discouraged. We can remind ourselves that God desires every good thing to come to us.

The words of Elisha came to pass just as he had prophesied. The woman became pregnant and gave birth to a son.

Years later, the boy was out in the fields with his father when he suddenly had a splitting headache. He collapsed and a reaper in the field carried him home to his mother. She held him on her lap to comfort him, but nothing helped. He died.

This Shunammite woman immediately asked her husband for use of a donkey and one of the servants, and she rode to Mount Carmel where she knew she would find Elisha. She implored him to return with her, and he agreed. When he arrived, he found the boy lying on his bed, lifeless. Elisha "went in, shut the door on the two of them and prayed to the LORD. Then he got on the bed and lay on the boy, mouth to mouth, eyes to eyes, hands to hands. As he stretched himself out upon him, the boy's body grew warm. Elisha turned away and walked back and forth in the room and then got on the bed and stretched out upon him once more. The boy sneezed seven times and opened his eyes" (2 Kings 4:33–35). The boy was restored to life and restored to his mother. What an amazing miracle, using amazing methods!

Was this mother filled with fear when her son died in her lap? I have no doubt she was doing everything she could *not* to panic. The good news is that she went immediately to the one place where she felt assured of receiving help.

If *you* are struggling with depression, *seek help!* Don't accept dark days and blue feelings as your new normal. The day you find yourself saying, "Something isn't right," is the day you need to make an appointment. Don't delay.

When this woman from Shunem first went to Elisha, she said, "As surely as the LORD lives and as you live, I will not leave you" (2 Kings 4:30). This woman had activated her will, and in the process she had activated her faith. She was believing for God to work on her behalf. Seek help with an attitude that you *are* going to be healed, and that you won't give up until you *are* healed!

As you pursue help for your depression, seek out someone

who is professionally qualified and who is someone you can trust personally. And then stick with the protocol that person prescribes for you. Don't flit from person to person or place to place. Don't start and stop therapeutic treatments without full consultation with your doctors or counselors. It often takes time for depression to heal and you need to be willing to walk out the entire process related to your healing.

Along the way, refuse to give up. There is healing ahead!

This woman's son wasn't healed fully the first time Elisha laid on top of him. But the *process* of healing unfolded nonetheless and the healing was eventually complete.

Look for evidence of God's healing process.
Refuse to give up on what God might do!

Believe for God's healing process to be at work in you *right now*, and look for it to progress until it comes to completion. Look for evidence of God's healing process. Refuse to give up on what God might do!

Identifying Your False Assumptions

Many of the lies the devil feeds us come packaged as "false assumptions." Four of those assumptions are especially potent.

False Assumption #1:
Everything in My Life Is a Mess

When a person begins to be depressed, all of life can seem dark and troubled. In truth, however, most problems seem to follow an eighty-twenty rule. Eighty percent of life is fine—it is functioning smoothly and the relationships are healthy. The problems are about twenty percent of life's whole.

It is important, I believe, for a person to recognize that not everything in life is falling apart. That can be a tendency if a major problem or crisis arises. If you focus only on the problems, without also recognizing the "good" aspects of your life, you can begin to see life as darker and more painful than it really is.

Many people have a tendency to focus on the storm cloud, not the sun that is creating a silver lining. Many women, myself included, tend to focus on what hasn't been done or what hasn't been accomplished rather than on what *has* been completed, accomplished, or produced.

It is also easy to see the failures and faults of others to the point that we lose sight of their successes and good qualities.

Keeping this eighty-twenty perspective can lead a person to conclude, "I don't need to change *everything* in my life and certainly not to change everything at the same time!"

My husband reminded me one time that all four wheels of a car rarely fall off at the same time, or even go flat at the same time! One flat can make you feel wobbly and even make the car difficult to steer or keep on the road. But . . . it is one flat! We can get it fixed and move forward. We don't need a new car . . . or a total revamping of life.

The eighty-twenty rule also keeps us from going to the extremes of "absolute" thinking:

- I'll never . . .
- It's all over . . .
- I will always . . .
- My children will always have . . .

Only God's Word is absolute.

False Assumption #2: The Past Is in the Past

Some women dismiss their past, saying almost lightly, "Well, that's all in the past." If the past is still defining any part of your life, then the past really isn't in the past. The old hurts are still alive in your mind and emotions.

If you find yourself still talking about the pain you felt . . . it is still the pain you are feeling.

If you find yourself still blaming someone about an event in the past . . . that event is still defining your responses today.

Recognize that a full release of the past is often the key to bouncing back.

A full release of the past is often the key to bouncing back.

The truth is we can't really forget anything—not really. But we can choose to learn from the past, ask God to help us apply those lessons to the present, and ask Him to show us how to walk forward in strength. If we don't learn from past failures, mistakes, or sins, then we continue to sorrow without hope and we apply the *pain* of the past to countless experiences in the present.

False Assumption #3:
I Know What That Person Is Up To

Maybe you do. But maybe you don't.

We often make faulty judgments, based upon our ability—or inability—to perceive accurately what certain behaviors and circumstances *really* mean. Virtually everybody I've ever met needs help to some degree when it comes to recognizing the difference between truth and lie, especially when it comes to behaviors that are very subtle or that are very cleverly disguised. We wouldn't be manipulated if we *knew* we were being manipulated. We wouldn't be shocked at the most extreme outcomes of violent or sinful behavior if we had seen the potential for that behavior early on.

I am absolutely in favor of people going to seminars and conferences that present insights into harmful patterns and early-onset warning symptoms. I also am aware that our perception is directly linked to what the Bible terms *discernment*. We need to ask God daily to help us discern fully what is happening around us, to be able to identify problems at early stages, and then avoid or confront those problems.

Some months ago I met a woman who was extremely angry. She was 100 percent convinced that someone had caused her to be fired from her job, and she was determined to find out the name of the person and take action. *And* she was 100 percent convinced that her pastor was spreading lies about her husband to drive them both away from the church. *And* she was 100 percent convinced that her son-in-law was cheating on her daughter and needed to be confronted about it.

Were all of these things happening? Perhaps. But with certainty I knew that the extreme anger she felt was the *main* problem she needed to confront.

Did this woman experience depression? Not immediately. But the day did come when she admitted to a mutual friend that she was losing her ability to function in the normal responsibilities of her life because she felt so angry so much of the time. Her friend suggested that she speak to a counselor in their city, and she did. This woman's anger had built up to the point of extreme frustration and discouragement, and she was on the path *toward* depression, perhaps closer than she ever realized.

False Assumption #4: My Fears Are "Normal"

Most of us need help in getting to the bottom of our fears. Fears are sometimes masked as feelings of uneasiness, dread, or suspicion. It is normal to feel fear about walking across a busy freeway at rush hour—our fear should keep us from stepping into the flow of traffic! It is also normal to be *concerned* about a trend of behavior or the potential of harm to ourselves or our loved ones. Concern should propel us to act and to seek preemptive solutions.

I once met a woman who told me that she had always had a deep fear of public speaking. She was a great conversationalist and could speak easily to three or four women sitting around a lunch table. If a group grew to the size of eight or more, she developed clammy hands and a dry mouth. She said at times she could hardly get out a word, even if she knew that she *should* say something.

This woman went to a communications expert and said, "I want you to help me." He gave her some very practical advice, but he also encouraged her to talk to a Christian counselor to explore possible reasons she felt this intense fear. She did and later said, "I learned so much! My fear was not shallow. Even though a fear of public speaking is one of the top five fears that most people admit to having, this is not a fear God desires in His children. Just think about the impact on our ability to share the Gospel. The more I learned about fears, and our tendency to accept fears as 'normal,' the more I could hardly wait to tell others about my experience and what I had learned from it—no matter how large the group!"

Was this woman depressed about her fear of public speaking? No, not directly. But she was frustrated by it to the point of becoming discouraged about it, and in feeling *those* emotions, she was on the path toward depression. How much better it is to stop the trend toward depression long before its darkness engulfs us.

The fears that are deep-seated within us, however, do not have a positive dimension to them. They cripple us emotionally. They paralyze us and keep us from fulfilling our God-given potential or from pursuing the dreams we know the Lord has planted in our hearts and minds.

Those fears are sometimes difficult to recognize, especially if we seem to have had the fear for many years or from early childhood. But your past isn't your past if it's still affecting your present.

It is vitally important for you to be able to identify a fear and call it what it is—and then to learn skills for getting rid of that fear.

Before a person can be fully free of deep fear, that person needs to be able to call the fear by name and then have help in making choices and decisions about how to walk free of the fear.

If you are struggling with longstanding paranoia, fear, or phobias—seek help. It is not God's desire for you to be bound up in ways that keep you from living out His plans and purposes for you.

No Shame in Seeking Help

Finally, let me say that there is no shame in admitting that you are depressed. Nor is there shame in seeking counseling or treatment for depression. Furthermore, depression is *not* an indicator of weak faith or spiritual immaturity.

A woman once said to me, "I did as you suggested and went away to breathe for a few days. I reaffirmed my faith and values and grew strength in what I believe. But I didn't bounce back from my depression. Rather, my spiritual retreat time gave me the *courage* to make an appointment with a Christian psychologist, keep that appointment, and then begin a bounce-back process. I'm not saying that the *breathe* and *believe* steps were ineffective. They were *very* effective! They set me on the path toward a full recovery from my depression—a process that continues to this day."

Anytime we face a problem, we are wise to acknowledge the problem and seek help for it. We are wise to pray and ask for God's help—certainly! But we are also wise to ask God to lead us to an expert with skills and experience related to our problem. I admit that I could pray for many hours about a *ping-ping-thunk* sound in my automobile and at the end of my long time in prayer be no closer to a solution—*unless* I am willing to hear the Lord speak to my heart, "Take your car to the dealership."

Never allow others—and do not allow yourself—to put a stigma on getting help for emotional, psychological, or relational problems. There are thousands of professional counselors out there who love God and bring Him into the helping process.

Four Steps for Walking Free

There are four steps that help a person walk free of depression.

Walk Out the Entire Process

First, choose to walk out the entire process: *breathe . . . believe . . .* and then *bounce back*. You need to give ample time to the first two stages before you try to bounce.

Take Baby Steps

Camille is a beautiful woman, divorced and with a child. She began using drugs many years ago and is a heroin addict in search of a lasting healing. She is the black sheep of her family, and she is sharply aware of that. She has come to several of our conferences. Her intent and heart is *sincere* in her desire to grow spiritually. She tends to take two steps forward, and then in the months that follow, she has a track record of taking one step back.

This might sound like discouraging news, but the *good* news is that the net effect over a year is still one step forward.

We must never discount the small changes that can build over time. Most of God's healing processes are incremental. This is especially true if a woman is coming out of a long history of abuse or an addiction, or out of a deep depression.

Don't Try to "Go It Alone" in Life

There's an old Jewish proverb that says, "He who goes too far alone, goes mad." We were meant to be in relationship with other people. We need people to listen to us, and we need to listen to others. We need people to care about us, and we have a need to extend care.

Reach out to:

- a person who might become your prayer partner, or who will be a faithful intercessor for you, your children, and your marriage;
- a person who will be a mentor to you, helping you learn skills or learn how to deal with various situations that are related to your work or ministry;
- a person who will be a steady source of encouragement to you.

Even as you reach out, open your life to be able to receive from others whom the Lord prompts to reach out to you. Trust the Lord to send others to encourage or to help you, usually at the time you need the encouragement or help the most.

I recently came home after a very difficult day—my mother had fallen and the doctors weren't certain if she would mend—and there at my house I found a little gift that a friend had left. It was a photo with words that were *exactly* what I needed to read. She had no idea what had happened to my mother that day, or how difficult my day had been. But God knew!

At times, I will turn on a Christian radio station and hear a song with lyrics that are very specifically what I need to hear most. I believe God prompted the person at the radio station to play that song just for me!

Keep Trying and Trusting

The only way a woman can learn to trust God more and more is to *try*. We learn to walk out our faith by trial and error, one step at a time, and with each step trusting God to help us *complete* that step. There's an old gospel song titled "Trust and Obey." The lyrics tell us that there is "no other way to be happy in Jesus." How true!

God promises us the ability to persevere and to grow in character as we remain obedient to Him in our hearts and trust Him to help us walk in obedience every day.

CHAPTER 6

Cure Your Loneliness by Adding Love

People are lonely because they build walls
instead of bridges.
—*Joseph Fort Newton*

Joyce found herself living in a place she had never imagined being—South America. Her husband had been transferred by his international corporation, and the entire family had moved for what they thought might be a three- or four-year overseas tour.

For Joyce's husband, Ben, the move was a validation of his work. Executives in his company were often sent on overseas assignments only to bounce back to the United States and occupy upper-management leadership over thousands of employees. Ben made the move with grace and ease. He found himself working daily at tasks he had mastered. Very quickly, he had some major successes in resolving problems.

Ben had another advantage. He had lived in South America for several years as a child of missionaries and he was fluent in Spanish. As a result of this early experience in his life, he had a strong comfort level with the Latin culture. All in all, he saw this new position as a wonderful challenge for which he had been fully prepared.

Joyce did *not* speak more than a few dozen phrases of Spanish. She had *not* grown up around Latinos, and much of the city in which she suddenly found herself was a flood of strange sounds, sights, and smells. She was *way* out of her comfort zone.

At first Joyce found the challenge of learning and adjusting to be exciting—difficult, but at the same time exotic and exhilarating. She found an English-speaking school and church for her family and enjoyed meeting some of the other expatriates living in the area, most of whom were American, but some of whom were from Canada and England.

Over time, however, a deep sense of homesickness set in. She missed the ease of the life she had known. She missed her family members and her friends and church friends. She missed little things: the ability to turn on the radio and hear the news in English, the ability to read and understand the signs and billboards of her new city, the availability of English-speaking programs on television, the pizza delivery guy and the drive-through hamburger stand and shopping without the need for bargaining.

She wondered at times, with small pangs of fear, what she would do if an emergency struck their family. She felt very uncertain about the resources available to her as a foreigner and about the people who might be able to help her and her family in a natural, political, or economic emergency. She admitted,

"I suddenly realized there was far more adjusting and learning I needed to do, far beyond being able to purchase food at the local market or knowing which bus to take to get to Ben's office."

Over time Joyce also discovered that the ex-pat English-speaking community—in general and at her church—was fairly fluid. She really couldn't count on people being present or available to her from one month to the next. So many seemed to be transferring in and transferring out of their roles and assignments abroad that it was difficult to keep up or feel settled. People seemed to leave without saying good-bye, or without giving any indication of a sooner-rather-than-later departure.

She said, "I was living in a major international city with more than a million other people, but apart from my children and husband, I felt that I was *alone*. Ben was spending long hours at work, and my son and daughter were spending as much time as they could with their new friends—struggling to adjust to the new culture and language as best they could. I felt adrift. I don't think there's anything more lonely than being surrounded by seemingly nice people and not feeling truly connected to them."

Joyce's situation was perhaps extreme, but the feelings she had were not unlike those I've heard expressed by many women in recent years. There seems to be a strong wave of disconnectedness in our society today. People are on the move. Children spend most of their awake hours *away* from home. Spouses are often moving in two different directions, rushing frantically to bridge home and work and often working extra-long hours just to keep up with career demands.

Some of the loneliest women I've met are women whose children have left the nest and who have lost a close connection to their husbands. One woman said with deep sorrow, "My husband and I both admit that we are estranged from each other. We don't want that to be the case, but we also are struggling to find our way back to the close and loving relationship we once had. We have acknowledged to each other that we need to spend more time together, but that's the big hurdle, isn't it? There's just no time for long, relaxed evenings spent on a porch swing watching the fireflies."

A Woman in a Lonely Role

A woman in the Bible who no doubt could have related well to Joyce was a young woman—a fairly young teenager, likely— who found herself in circumstances that must have seemed both strange and overwhelming to her.

Her name was Hadassah. She was an orphan girl living in ancient Persia, which we would know today as Iran. We don't know how or when her parents died, but the Bible does tell us that they were deceased. She had been taken in by an older relative who was raising her as his own daughter. His name was Mordecai and he may have been an uncle or older cousin.

I believe it is important to recognize that Hadassah was an orphan. Orphans, as well as those whose parents abandon them in some way when they are young, often admit to having very deep and abiding feelings of loneliness later in life. It is also important to recognize that Hadassah likely lived in a very sheltered, small community—with virtually no ties to the large cosmopolitan culture just miles from her front door.

Hadassah was Jewish. The Jews were a very small segment of the population in Persia, and while they were close to one another, they had very few relationships with those outside their own communities.

One day a man came to Hadassah's home and spoke to her guardian, asking to take Hadassah to the king's palace. The man had been part of a contingent sent to find the "fairest of the fair" young maidens in the land. This man wanted Hadassah to audition to be the next queen of Persia! Mordecai really had no option except to agree that Hadassah could go. At the king's palace, Hadassah was given a Persian name: Esther.

Esther wasn't the only young woman to arrive in the palace and begin a twelve-month beauty program in preparation for an audience with the king. Many others, all of whom were considered "lovely in form and features," had been brought to the palace. Esther, however, as far as we can tell from Scripture, was the only Jewish girl there.

Can you imagine how lonely and isolated she must have felt at this point? She was a *long* way from anything and anyone she knew.

Esther no doubt learned quickly *why* a new queen was being sought. The former queen had been summoned by the king to appear in her finest royal garments at a banquet he was hosting for the most powerful men throughout his kingdom. The summons came after the men at the banquet were thoroughly drunk. Vashti, the queen, had no interest in being paraded before a crowd of leering, jeering drunks. She refused to appear. Those in power saw this as a great affront to the king and to the status of men in the kingdom, and they tricked the king into forcing her out of her position as queen. Although the king later regretted his actions, he was kept by his own laws from reversing his banishment of Vashti from her throne. And thus, the search was on for a new queen to replace her.

The Bible tells us that the keeper of the king's harem was a man named Hegai. No details are given about Hegai, but we do know from historical documents that the men who were put in charge of royal harems were nearly always eunuchs, often prisoners of war from other cultures or nations. These men had been castrated but kept alive because they had certain skills, management abilities, or pleasant personalities. These men often became trusted and valuable servants. If this was the case in Hegai's life, he was likely just as isolated, lonely, and out of his element as Esther.

For reasons we aren't told, Hegai was drawn to Esther in a special way, and she won his favor. He provided her with the best beauty treatments and special foods, assigned seven maids from the king's palace to her, and moved her and her maids to the best place in the harem.

Esther was not allowed during this year of "preparation" to talk with Mordecai directly or to leave the palace grounds. Daily, however, Mordecai went to a courtyard near the harem to hear what he could about Esther's welfare. She likely knew that he was nearby, even if she had no contact with him.

The time came for Esther to go to the king. She relied completely on Hegai's advice about what to wear and what to take with her to the king's chambers, and she no doubt heard and received his advice about how to behave once she was with the king. She went to the king as a virgin and the next morning was directed to a different part of the harem where the concubines were housed. That part of the harem was expected to be her home for the rest of her life, unless the king called for her specifically.

All of this to say Esther's isolation and loneliness were not temporary. Once she left the home of Mordecai, she was separated from her people—from the other Jews, from her religious customs, from her culture—*permanently*. There would be no going back.

Esther was in an even more isolated position than Joyce in South America. Joyce always knew in the back of her mind that she could buy an airline ticket and fly home to family and friends and everything culturally familiar. Esther was stuck. After her night with the king, she was not returned to the part of the harem supervised by Hegai, but rather to an area supervised by a man named Shaashgaz. That meant that the one trusted friend she appeared to have made inside the palace walls was no longer in communication with her.

Amazing events unfolded. "The king was attracted to Esther more than to any of the other women, and she won his favor and approval more than any of the other virgins" (Esther 2:17). The king placed the queen's crown upon her head! A holiday was proclaimed throughout all the provinces of Persia. Esther was now Queen Esther.

Throughout this entire process, which lasted more than a year, Esther had not revealed to anyone in the palace that she was Jewish. (See Esther 2:1–20 for this portion of Esther's story.)

Personal Secrets Can Deepen Loneliness

I have learned through the years from many women that personal secrets can deepen loneliness. When a woman has a secret about herself or her past that she knows might be dangerous or damaging for her to reveal, she tends to become defensive and guarded, which only makes her less approachable and less trusting. Her secret makes it more difficult for her to be a friend or to receive friendship.

Joyce in South America had no secrets, but a woman named Ginger did.

Ginger had grown up very poor and had been the victim of incest. Her abuser had been her stepfather, who routinely raped Ginger from the time she was ten years old until she was fifteen, when she ran away from home.

When Ginger left home, she ran far and fast. She ended up more than a thousand miles away, where a woman she met at a café offered her a room and a bath. Ginger was so exhausted and so tired of running that she accepted the offer. A few days later she learned that the woman ran a brothel and Ginger was perceived to be her next prostitute in residence.

Ginger ran again, but not before stealing money and jewelry from the madam who had attempted to enslave her. She hitchhiked to a city forty miles away, rented a room, bought a new dress and shoes, and the next day got a job as a secretary. She had learned to type before her freshman year of high school and she was willing to work hard. Nobody questioned her age, which she had lied about. She worked her way up from the typing pool to an executive secretary's position, and along the way attracted the attention of an executive from a subsidiary company who came periodically for appointments with her boss. They dated, fell in love, and married.

Ginger began to attend the church of her new husband's family, accepted the Lord, and happily settled into what seemed like a fairy-tale life of being the wife of a godly man who provided a home and a new social status for her.

The last thing in the world that Ginger wanted was for someone from her past to recognize her, or for people to ask too many questions about her family, her upbringing, or her education. She added a layer of lies in telling her husband that her parents had died and that she had gone to secretarial school rather than college. She was a good student of behavior and quickly learned the manners and protocols of a social class far higher than that of her childhood.

She said later, "I was happy that I wasn't stuck in the sins of my childhood, but I was also unhappy. I felt as if there was a glass wall between me and others I met at church, or at social outings with my husband and his family. I had created a web of lies around myself that kept me quieter and more isolated than I *wanted* to be. But I didn't dare let anyone know my secrets."

The day came, as you might imagine, when someone from Ginger's past did appear. As the truth came out about her past, Ginger "died of embarrassment a thousand times." Fortunately for her, her husband and his family forgave Ginger for her lies and for her past sins. "It could have been so much worse," she said. "They could have shamed me or rejected me or held my past sins over my head, but they didn't. In forgiving me, they allowed me truly to discover *myself* for the first time in my life. I was free to begin to explore my own values, opinions, and abilities. Most important, I was free to forgive myself and trust God to make me and mold me according to the way He created me."

Ginger was encouraged by her mother-in-law to see a counselor to help her in forgiving herself and discovering more about her own self. This counselor suggested that she go on a women's four-day retreat to begin to explore what it might be like to share more fully with other women in an atmosphere of God's love. It was Ginger's time to breathe.

"I didn't know anybody at that retreat," Ginger said. "But I sensed tremendous love from the people in charge of the retreat, and I also sensed that many of the others who were there had been victims of abuse or had experienced deep troubles in their past. We all seemed wounded in some way. The leaders of the retreat encouraged us to see this time apart as a time to rest and to heal from the sorrows of our own pasts. That sounded so good to me!"

The women were encouraged to take long walks on the estate where the retreat was held. They were treated to various spa treatments—mud baths and massages included. They met in small groups to explore topics that were both fun and serious. They were treated like royal guests at mealtimes and in their accommodations.

"I would never have thought that four days could do so much for me, or for the other women at that event. God met us in an amazing way. I had been born again spiritually during a prayer service a couple of years before, but this weekend I really felt as if something came alive in my emotions and in my psyche. I begin to embrace *Ginger* and to like her and to want to share her with the other women around me."

The retreat was also a time for Ginger to learn to voice what she believed. She found several Scriptures during that weekend that became what she later called "foundation stones" for her life. She said, "I had heard about God's love before that weekend, but at the retreat I really began to *believe* that God loved *me*. He loved me just the way I was, but He also loved me so much that He wasn't going to leave me just the way I was. He was going to grow me and refine me to become the woman He knew I *truly* was."

Ginger was so blessed by what happened at the retreat that she asked her counselor what she might do to thank the women who ran the retreat. She said, "I even volunteered to go and help them in the garden or to clean at the estate house . . . for no charge."

In the end, Ginger did work with the retreat center and she became one of the leaders there. She regularly shares her story at retreats and has opportunities to have personal conversations and prayer with those who are learning to breathe and affirm what they believe.

She has said, "I once was ashamed of my past, but today I see my life as a huge miracle. God transformed my past into my glorious present. And if He did that for me, I know He can and will do that for others. My life isn't perfect . . . but I know my future will be! Someday I will be with the Lord in paradise and that's when perfection will become a reality. Every woman should have that hope!"

I think Queen Esther would have liked Ginger and admired her transformation.

Esther's Secret Revealed

Esther's secret about being a Jew was an act of self-preservation on her part. This was especially true after Mordecai uncovered the plot of a wicked man named Haman who hated all Jews and sought to annihilate them from Persia. The king had elevated Haman to a position higher than all of the other nobles in his court, and Haman came to expect people to bow to him and pay him homage. Mordecai refused to kneel down or pay him honor. That was equal to worship in Mordecai's mind, and Mordecai knew that no Jew was ever to worship another human being. Haman discovered that Mordecai was a Jew, and thus he transferred his hatred toward Mordecai to all Jews.

Haman went to the king and said,

> There is a certain people dispersed among the peoples in all the provinces of your kingdom who keep themselves separate. Their customs are different from those of all other people, and they do not obey the king's laws; it is not in the king's best interest to tolerate them. If it pleases the king, let a decree be issued to destroy them, and I will give ten thousand talents of silver to the king's administrators for the royal treasury. (Esther 3:8–9)

"'Keep the money,'" the king said to Haman, "'and do with the people as you please'" (Esther 3:11).

When Mordecai heard about the edict that meant his demise, as well as the death of all other Jews in Persia, he put on sackcloth and ashes and sat at the entrance to the palace. Esther summoned one of the king's eunuchs assigned to attend her and ordered him to find out why Mordecai had done this. Mordecai sent back word of Haman's actions and urged her to go to the king and beg for mercy for her people.

Esther sent a second message to Mordecai explaining that she had not been summoned by the king during the previous thirty days and she could not just go to him without a summons from him. Mordecai replied, "Do not think that because you are in the king's house you alone of all the Jews will escape. For if you remain silent at this time, relief and deliverance for the Jews will arise from another place, but you and your father's family will perish. And who knows but that you have come to your royal position for such a time as this?" (Esther 4:13–14).

Esther sent back word to Mordecai to gather the Jews in Susa together and to fast for her. She would also fast, along with her maids. And she would go to the king, even if it meant her death. She said, "If I perish, I perish" (Esther 4:16). This was not necessarily an indication of futility or anticipated doom, but rather a clear statement that her life would definitely be on the line either way—if she didn't go to the king, she would likely be killed. If she *did* go to the king too boldly, she could also lose her life as the queen.

We know, of course, that when Esther appeared just outside the king's court, dressed in her finest royal garments, he looked with favor on her and he accepted an invitation to a banquet in her chambers. The night of the first banquet, he offered her tremendous favor, but she asked only that he return the following night for a second feast. At that second banquet, when the king offered her anything she desired, even up to half of his kingdom, Esther replied:

> If I have found favor with you, Your Majesty, and if it pleases you, grant me my life—this is my petition. And spare my people—this is my request. For I and my people have been sold to be destroyed, killed and annihilated. If we had merely been sold as male and female slaves, I would have kept quiet, because no such distress would justify disturbing the king. (Esther 7:3–4)

When the king asked, "Who is he? Where is the man who has dared to do such a thing?" Esther said, "The adversary and enemy is this vile Haman."

In the end, Haman was hung on the very gallows he had built to hang Mordecai.

Esther asked the king to send out an edict overturning the dispatches of Haman, and the king did so. He included in his edict the right of the Jews to assemble and to protect themselves against any persecutors.

Mordecai was given the signet ring of the king and he became the second most powerful man in all of Persia. He enjoyed a position of prominence in the palace and a growing reputation throughout the land, becoming more and more powerful. (See Esther 3:1 through 9:1 for the complete story.)

Courage That Produced a Lasting Legacy

Queen Esther and Mordecai worked together to establish an annual festival to mark "the time when the Jews got relief from their enemies" and when "their sorrow was turned into joy and their mourning into a day of celebration" (Esther 9:22). The festival was to be observed with feasting, the giving of food gifts to one another, and special gifts to the poor. The Feast of Purim is still celebrated by the Jewish people today.

From what we read in the last chapters of Esther, Esther had many opportunities for fellowship with Mordecai and her people after this crisis had ended. Her loneliness appears to have been fully reversed.

Talk about a bounce back!

I encourage you to consider the three days that Esther and her maids fasted as a time of *breathing* for them. They set themselves apart, even as a death sentence hung in the air. Esther's maids may not even have been aware of the reason for the fast, but Esther certainly was. This was a time of deep reflection for her as she sought God's wisdom about just the right way to approach the king, her husband . . . and just the right way to reveal the wickedness of the king's most trusted advisor . . . and just the right words to ensure the ongoing life of her beloved Mordecai, her people, and herself. It certainly would have been a time for Esther to recall and reaffirm all that she had been trained to believe about God, about His people, and about His commandments.

In later years, Esther no doubt reflected many times upon just how merciful God had been, and about how God had *used* her, and about how her time of isolation and loneliness resulted in a tremendous benefit and blessing.

What can we conclude from Esther's story as being applicable to us today?

God Does Not Desire That Any Person Be Lonely

God may allow us to go into seclusion for a time, but that time is never expected to be permanent. God desires for us to be in fellowship with others, and that fellowship is to include agreement about our deep values and beliefs as followers of Christ. The Bible tells us that even those who are single are "set" in families by the Lord—He provides others to love us and for us to love (Psalm 68:6).

Let me tell you what happened to Joyce.

I mentioned earlier that Joyce always knew in the back of her mind that she could return to the United States anytime she chose to do so. That was actually part of her agreement with her husband as they anticipated a move to South America. Joyce eventually *did* exercise that option. She wasn't intending to make a permanent move home, but rather to spend a two-month summer vacation with her children so they might visit both sets of grandparents and old friends.

While they were in the United States, Joyce took a few days for herself to reflect and reevaluate her life. It was her time to breathe. She went with a close friend to the mountain home of her friend's sister and brother-in-law. There, with the beauty of nature all around her, she had plenty of opportunity to relax and spend long stretches of time in quiet prayer and Bible reading. It was a great time for her to ask, "Why does God have *me* in South America?" Joyce had a good idea why God had her husband, Ben, there, but she wanted affirmation that God had a plan and purpose specifically for her. She reflected on what she deeply believed about God's plans and purposes for her life, and also upon the opportunities that she may have overlooked in her new South American home.

When Joyce returned to South America, she asked at both her children's school and at their church home if there were oppor-tunities for her to volunteer. Of course! She ended up teaching a

Sunday school class for preschoolers. "The hugs from these little ones were so special to me," she later recounted. "It was pure joy to see their faces light up when Miss Joyce came into the room!" She was given more than a volunteer job at the school. She was asked to be the administrative aide to the principal, who quickly discovered Joyce's artistic and musical talents and assigned her to be the school's art and music teacher. Joyce had majored in elementary education in college, so she dusted off her diploma and dove in.

As part of her work at the school, Joyce became better acquainted with a large number of artists and musicians in the city and developed new intercultural friendships that continue to this day. She has sponsored several of these musicians and artists for concerts and showings now that she and Ben are back home after *ten years* in South America. And, by the way, her Spanish is fluent.

Joyce bounced back in an amazing way, one that set her on a whole new life direction. Again, I think Esther would have approved!

God Desires That We Turn to Him When We Feel Lonely

He wants to minister directly to us with His loving presence and tender mercies. "But I don't *feel* God," you may be saying. I understand that. Our goal, however, should be to learn to be still in God's presence as we invite Him to reveal Himself to us. This may not happen overnight, but eventually most people begin to take comfort in the silence of prayerful contemplation of the Scriptures and in their adoration of the Lord.

Adoration is a spiritual discipline we don't talk much about in the church these days, but it has a longstanding place of high value in the history of the church. Adoration is quiet reflection on the goodness and greatness of God—on His glory, His splendor, His majesty. Adoration involves shutting out all other thoughts, sounds, and influences to focus, focus, focus on the Lord. It isn't easy to do this! In fact, for some of us it takes a *lot* of practice, especially the requirement for reining in all other thoughts related to ourselves and the world around us. But adoration is a key to experiencing a deep intimacy with the Lord.

God Desires That We Love Others

God desires that we open ourselves up to the possibility He has sent or is sending us people to love that we are not presently loving.

Read me carefully on this: I am certainly *not* talking about any kind of romantic fling or love affair with someone other than your spouse. I am *not* talking about abandoning any of the current relationships that are in need of your love—your children, your parents, your close friends, or people who are part of a ministry in which you are involved. A problem I have witnessed repeatedly is the problem of "looking for love in all the wrong places." There is a right and wrong way for adding more love to our lives.

What I am suggesting is that love can take many different forms and be for different times and seasons in our life. Love is God's foremost method for expanding His kingdom. If you asked me for the key to evangelism, the growth of any body of Christ, the building up of the downtrodden, the healing of the brokenhearted, and the establishment of God's justice for all suffering in this world, I could sum it up in one word: *love*.

Let me assure you that even if you are lonely and feel that *you* are in need of love . . . you have love to give.

Let me further assure you that even if you have been disappointed in love relationships in the past . . . yes, you *still* have love to give, and yes, you *do* have a need to give love!

Yes, you *still* have love to give, and yes, you *do* have a need to give love!

Let me assure you that God can and will bring across your path the unloved ones who need to become *your* new loved ones, if you ask Him to do so.

More and More Love to Give

I have never met a woman who could say, "I have absolutely all the love I can contain in my heart." We always seem to have a capacity for more.

It might be the capacity to love another child.

Or make a new friend.

Or find a new way of expressing love to an old friend.

I suspect that if God gave a little gift card with His Word, it might read, "Just add love."

You may want to devote a long weekend just to breathing in God's love, searching the Scriptures, and asking the Lord how you might breathe His love into someone who is even more lonely or isolated than you are. I can almost guarantee you that the Lord will bring some person or some situation to your mind and give you an enthusiasm or a sense of conviction that you need to reach out and give what you can.

Love is a word of affection in our world, but in Bible terms *love* is almost synonymous with *giving*. When we love, we have a strong desire to give. When we give, we find ourselves expanding in our capacity for and fervency of love. Love is expressed in giving. Giving creates greater feelings of love. The process is a cycle and it makes a whole.

Love—give—love—give—love . . .

Love is expressed in giving. Giving creates greater feelings of love. The process is a cycle and it makes a whole.

Joyce began to give of her talent to school and church children. She got back love, and out of her love she gave and gave and gave.

Ginger gave of her time to help out at a retreat center, and she gave with love. She grew in her ability to love and in opportunities to give. She loved and gave and loved and gave.

Esther didn't start out asking her husband to give to her. She invited him to dinner . . . and then invited him to dinner again. Her love for her people motivated her to take a risk and *give*. And in the end, it was this approach of giving first that even more deeply won her husband's heart and saved her people.

I don't know where God might lead you to love and give, but there certainly are countless venues for you to do both.

You may feel drawn to those who are in need of food and shelter and a new beginning—perhaps at a homeless shelter or at a refugee shelter that ministers to the victims of natural catastrophes. You may feel drawn to a nursing home or retirement center. You may feel led to look into the opportunities to be a foster parent or a mentor to a young person who has recently aged out of the foster-care system.

The Lord may lead you to give of your talents to a new ministry. Or to a new mentoring program in your church. Or to teach children some of the skills you have developed in your life—perhaps in art and music as Joyce did, or perhaps in areas of drama, foreign language learning, tutoring in math or reading, or a wide variety of other areas where children and young people can benefit greatly from "an older adult besides Mom" who is available to listen, love, and give.

A woman shared something profound with me not long ago. She said, "I was lonely as long as I was inside my house thinking about my own lack of love and lack of friends. The turnaround for me came when I opened the front door and walked outside. I saw a few people across the street clearing the vacant lot there and digging up the soil to plant a garden. I went over and introduced myself and asked if I could help. That was five years ago. I've been helping plant and sustain community gardens across my city since that day. Lonely? Not a bit.

"As long as I was waiting for someone to come into my life and zap loneliness out of my heart, I was stuck. When I made the choice to walk into the lives of others, loneliness disappeared."

A big part of loving is also forgiving—which is a form of *giving*.

The Gift of Forgiveness

Loneliness often goes hand in glove with ongoing, often very deep, feelings of resentment, jealousy, bitterness, and anger. The more a person sits alone and stews about past instances of hurt and injustice, the more a person is prone to these highly negative emotions.

A dear friend of mine was abandoned by her husband after two decades of marriage. There was no other woman involved, but my friend suspected there might be. She simply couldn't come to grips with any other reason why her husband might have left her, and with so little sorrow over the end of their marriage. She had deep resentment for his having turned her life upside down, and over time her anger and bitterness became like sludge at the bottom of her soul.

She was also angry with those who had been mutual friends of their marriage who seemed to side with her husband. She was especially angry that her husband's boss continued to keep him employed. The boss was their pastor, and my friend felt doubly betrayed and as if she had no church home. She confided in me, "It never dawned on me that our pastor might take sides. I felt as if I had no pastor who could pray with me or counsel me *fairly*. Not only did I lose my marriage, but my church home."

For months and months, my friend was inconsolable. She shut herself in and only rarely agreed to go out to an event with me. Her loneliness was deeply embedded in an unforgiving heart.

The good news is that the day came when my friend finally admitted to the Lord that she didn't *want* to forgive but she knew she *needed* to forgive. She didn't forgive because she had an emotional desire to forgive or feelings of forgiveness. She forgave as an act of her will. She understood that forgiveness is a command God expects each of us to obey.

Forgiveness is a command God expects each of us to obey.

She told me later, "I heard a Bible teacher say that forgiveness is a command. Jesus didn't make it an option. He said, 'Forgive, and you will be forgiven.' The opposite meaning is clear: 'Don't forgive, and you won't be forgiven.' So, solely on the basis of that, I *chose* to forgive. It wasn't easy, but it was *required*."

I would like to tell you that my friend's heart was softened and cleansed and restored in a day. It wasn't. She found that she needed to forgive multiple times over the next few months, but the day did come when she not only fully experienced God's forgiveness, but she forgave *herself* fully. And it was at that point that her loneliness began to lift. She began to reach out to others. She went to her former pastor and they had a good time of prayer together, which was a healing experience for her. She went to family and friends and asked them to forgive her and they did. Little by little, she emerged from the isolation she had created for herself with her unforgiving anger, bitterness, and resentment.

Ask yourself today if your loneliness is linked to your own unforgiving heart. If so, make today the day you ask the Lord to help you forgive.

Have you built a wall around yourself that is now isolating you from friendships and opportunities the Lord has for you? Make today the day you open your life to the new "love relationships" God has in your future.

Are you holding people at arm's length and thus generating isolation and its feelings of loneliness? Perhaps the time has come to reach out.

You will not only benefit personally, but you just may save the lives of many others as you give to them and show them God's mercy and love.

Give forgiveness a try! Don't swallow the hurt, anger, and pain. Release it. Cancel the debt. It will change your future.

CHAPTER 7

A Stronger You

God looked over everything he had made;
it was so good, so very good!
—*Genesis 1:31 (MSG)*

Will we ever get to the point where we no longer need to
bounce back?

Yes.

In heaven.

Until then, we are going to face repeated challenges in
our lives that are likely going to become new opportunities to
breathe, believe, and *bounce back.* Anytime you take a serious
hit in life—suffer a major disappointment or loss—you will be
wise to take the time to retreat into the Lord, reaffirm your faith,
and seek God's guidance. There is no limit to the number of
times a person is allowed to step back to breathe and believe as
preparatory steps to bouncing back.

But even more than bouncing *back,* these opportunities are
going to enable you to bounce *forward.*

There are many things that we seem to lose that are worth
fighting to reclaim. There are other things that we are better off
letting go.

And there are some things that we are to reach for, but to date, we have not even begun to entertain the pursuit of those dreams or to set those goals. The very idea of God's next step for us hasn't yet entered our hearts or minds!

Getting Back What's Been Lost

As you set time apart to breathe and to reaffirm what you believe, ask the Lord to help you identify in a clear and concise way what it is that you believe you have lost.

If You Have Lost Material Things . . .

Ask the Lord if those things are items He considers to be important for the fulfillment of your plan and purpose on the earth. If so, ask the Lord to use His methods to replace them in His timing. (Don't be surprised if He restores to you something even *better* than what you lost.) Above all, ask the Lord to supply what you *need*—not only now, but in the future.

If You Have Lost a Relationship . . .

Ask the Lord to heal your broken heart and help you through the grieving process. Not all relationships are lost by death. A divorce or a broken engagement or any other type of relationship that is called to an end by another person can be a lost relationship.

Ask the Lord if He desires for you to pray and wait, in anticipation that the former relationship might be restored or renewed.

Recognize that it takes time for a heart to heal emotionally, especially if bitterness, anger, rejection, or other forms of emotional pain have been experienced. Don't be too quick to jump into new relationships or into an overly active social life. You may put yourself in a position of experiencing even greater emotional pain.

At the same time, do expect to heal and, in God's timing, to love again. Be open to the possibilities of *new* relationships that can satisfy your longing to be valued, appreciated, and cared for.

If You Lost a Job . . .

Ask the Lord to give you an even better job. The Lord alone knows the specific job that will make maximum use of your abilities, talents, and energy. He alone knows the job that will give you great fulfillment. And He alone knows how to hook you up with people who will value you as a person, be generous toward you, challenge you to do your best, and reward you for your finest efforts.

If You Have Lost Your Health . . .

Ask the Lord to restore it! Do not resign yourself to being an invalid or to being less than well. Work hard to gain back your strength, energy, mobility, and zest for living. Ask God to do for you what you cannot do to be whole. Look for strength and healing to come step by step, over time. Take charge of your attitude and refuse to think like a sick person or to see yourself as the victim of a disease. God is still in the miracle-working business and His desire is always to make us whole in spirit, soul, and body.

If You Have Lost a Sense of Purpose . . .

Ask the Lord to renew in you an awareness that, no matter what has happened, God still has a future prepared for you. If you have lost all hope related to your future and the dreams you once had, remember He has something more for you to do, and definitely something more for you to be as His beloved child on this earth. Ask Him to reveal to you at least the next step of His plan and purpose.

Renew your own understanding of the gifts and talents God has built into your life. There are some abilities you have had from birth—things you have always been good at or enjoyed doing. Explore those abilities with renewed awareness that they were a gift from God and that God may still have a purpose for giving you the particular abilities you have.

Revisit your dreams and goals. Something may not have turned out exactly as you planned—but there are nearly always more than a few paths to get to a goal. One method may have not worked, but that doesn't mean the goal is wrong. The economic environment may have changed, your location may be different, or your resources may have shifted, but none of this automatically means that new factors might not exist *now* that God can use for your good.

Reaffirm that God loves you and values you, so much that He sent His Son to die so you can live an eternal life and a blessed life between now and eternity (John 3:16). God has not abandoned you, even if it seems to you that everybody else has. God has not given up on you, even if you have given up on yourself!

The Same . . . or Better?

Some things we lose are better left lost. We don't like to consider the reality that we are better off without the things we have lost, but that's the truth at times.

Some things we lose are better left lost.

The things that you have lost may have become idols in your life without you even realizing it. They may have been robbing you of time and energy that God desires for you to channel into new activities and relationships that hold the promise of even greater blessing.

A woman once told me, "We worked for years to build a nice second home at the beach. We collected items for that home and stored them in our attic and basement. The time came when we could afford to build our retreat, and for the first few months after it was completed, we had a huge amount of fun hosting our friends for weekend getaways. And then it hit us: the time we were going to our home at the beach was the *weekend*. We were absent from church and Sunday school more times than we were present. We faced the truth that we really didn't want to give up church for a house by the sea. We spent a weekend at the lake by ourselves, asking God what we should do, and He made it clear that we were to adjust our priorities and find a way to give our vacation home to others and use it only occasionally ourselves."

Another couple discovered massive foundation problems at the very large new house they had recently purchased after a fire badly damaged their former home. Contractors told them that more than thirty pilings would be required to stabilize the house on the shifting clay. "We had to face a very hard reality," this couple shared with me. "We had told ourselves that we wanted a newer and bigger house. We had not, however, asked God about the purchase of this particular house. We consider it a miracle from God's hand that He arranged for the sale to be annulled. What we had thought we wanted was not at all what was best for us. God led us to a different property—smaller and older than we had initially desired, but in the course of moving into *that* house, we discovered neighbors and a neighborhood church that were just right for us."

If God does not restore to you *precisely* what you believe should be restored, ask God to have *His* way and to give you what *He* wants you to have. God knows what is best for you, and if you are willing to receive His best, you can count on His giving it!

One woman told me that it was only *after* her husband had divorced her that she learned about the many affairs he had during their marriage, and about the sexually transmitted disease that he had contracted. It was God's provision that he left when he did, because that sexually transmitted disease had not infected *her*. If he had remained another two months, it likely would have.

Another woman told me that it was only *after* her son ran away that he found himself hitting bottom emotionally to the degree that he cried out to God for help—for the first time in his life. He told his mother later, "It took a week in a county jail for me to become sober enough to face my life squarely and realize that I needed the Lord." Mom said, "I would never have wanted or planned that experience for my son, but God was in charge all the time. He came home a different young man—in many ways the man I always knew he *could* be if he would let the Lord into his life."

Don't be too quick to discount a circumstance as bad until you have given it to God—at which point you will likely discover that it's just the kind of bad He uses at times to create something *good*.

And don't be too quick to expect or demand that God give you back exactly what you lost or what you claim to want, in exactly the way you want it or on the timetable you set for restoration. God *is* at work at all times, but His timing is perfect. He is not only preparing goodness for your future, but for all others who are involved in that future goodness.

There's a joke that asks, "What happens when you play a country-western song in reverse?" The answer: "You get your pickup back, you get your girlfriend back, you get your money back . . . "

In life, of course, there are never any guarantees that we will get back *exactly* what we have lost. God's promise is that He will provide all that we need and will restore all things that are necessary for the ongoing fulfillment of His purposes for our life. He will be the faithful Source of all we need.

We can trust God, however, for certain things:

- We can get back our ability to dream.
- We can get back our anointing.
- We can get back spiritual strength, peace, and joy.
- We can get our "fight" back.

I've always had fight in me. Not a desire to fight with other people, but rather a desire to fight against the devil and to claim all that God has for me and my family. Jesus called the devil a thief (John 10:10). I'm not at all interested in having the devil steal anything that is rightfully mine as a child of God!

Relax and Enjoy the Process

Many women feel pressure to move too quickly out of a tragedy or painful experience. We live in an instant-gratification, microwave, and immediate-results world!

I cannot tell you how many women I've talked with who confide to me they are feeling pressured to forgive when they don't feel like forgiving, pressured to date after a spouse's death or a divorce when they don't feel like dating, or pressured to make a major change in their life—their schedule, their location, their job—when they are still trying to define and accept the change.

Breathing is a time to step back from the pressures and rest, consider, and contemplate. It is a time to search out answers to the nagging questions that often seem too big or too deep to address in the midst of a break-neck schedule surrounded by others who mean well but often aren't very helpful.

Change often involves an emotional balancing act. We must be willing to change and to move forward in our lives in ways that are positive and helpful. We must resist, however, a tendency to change solely for the sake of change, or to make changes too hastily without enough serious reflection. We especially must resist change that comes as a result of others pressuring us to change.

When we breathe, we take a step back to evaluate.

We acknowledge our pain and disappointment with life.

We purposefully slow down.

So many women who have experienced huge disappointments or troubles feel as if their mind is racing, often in a circle. There are so many *why*, *what if*, and *what now* questions that seem to demand answers, which may not yet be clear. Breathing is a time to turn off the endless questioning and just rest, and over time begin to *accept* in very simple terms what is.

Breathing is a time to fall limply into the arms of a loving heavenly Father who doesn't scold us or instruct us, but simply holds us and comforts us.

Scientists are telling us that "deep breathing" several times a day is one of the best things we can do for our physical health. Slow, deep breathing is also therapeutic in the emotional and spiritual realm.

Rather than ask *why*, *what if*, or *what now* questions, we are wise to ask ourselves:

- What have been my priorities?
- Who have I added to my life—and are these relationships helpful or harmful?
- How has my daily routine changed?

- What new interests have I developed?
- Have I taken on new goals, responsibilities, or obligations?
- Am I experiencing more or less joy . . . more or less inner peace . . . more or less fulfillment and satisfaction?
- What disappointments have I experienced—and how have I dealt with them?
- What lies have I believed about the degree to which life "owes" me happiness?
- Do I seem to make the same mistakes again and again?
- Am I in better or worse health than I was this time last year?
- Have I been consistent in my relationship with the Lord?

Refuse to draw conclusions too quickly. Remain thoughtful. Wait for the Lord to reveal His answers.

The Nature of Your Retreat

Consider linking the nature of your retreat to the nature of your loss. Put yourself into a position to gain new information or new insights related to your loss or to the pain you have been experiencing.

Take your Bible and a small concordance to help you find passages of God's Word that relate directly to your situation.

Focus on scriptures and affirmations of believing that relate to what you are anticipating God will restore to you.

Your time to breathe is not a time to get the opinions of others. It is time to get *God's* opinion. Turn off your phone and stay off the Internet or your social media outlets for a while. Seek God's presence. Do your utmost to discern God's directives.

You may, however, benefit from taking inspirational reading materials with you. I encourage you to read the life stories of women who have gone through experiences similar to the one you are facing.

When it comes to reading the Scriptures, I encourage you to read aloud to yourself the words of Jesus. It helps if you have a Bible that shows Jesus' words in red ink.

- Read aloud the miracles of Jesus.
- Believe with renewed faith that Jesus is the same yesterday, today, and forever (Hebrews 13:8).
- Listen. And then listen even more.
- Remind yourself repeatedly about God's greatness and goodness.

Nothing is too difficult for God to do. He can give you sufficient grace to see you through the most difficult time.

Nothing overrides God's ability to govern time. He can act quickly on your behalf—or impart to you patience to wait for His slow-brewing plan to unfold.

Nobody is beyond God's ability to move people into the right place and time to be of maximum assistance or blessing to you.

An Ongoing Life of Renewal

The Lord promises to refine us and to renew us.

Both refining and renewing are lifelong processes. These

processes take time and do not end until we take our final breath and enter into His presence.

This means there is *always* a good reason for us to hold on to our hope and to keep trusting God to take us to the next level of spiritual maturity and blessing He has already prepared for us to occupy.

Refining and renewing are lifelong processes . . .
Faith and love are renewable resources.

We never run out of potential. And God's promise is that we will never run out of His presence.

Faith and love are renewable resources. Tap into them and see the spring they give to your step and the zest they give to your life as you bounce back and experience a breakthrough into your future.

A Daily Dose of Bs!

Can a person develop a routine in which she has time to breathe and affirm what she believes on a daily basis? Or perhaps a weekly basis?

I think it is much easier to develop such a routine if a person has had an initial extended time to breathe and believe—a weekend, week, or several days away to gain perspective and regain her spiritual and emotional footing. That longer experience can be a touchstone as a woman takes a short period of time daily to be alone, be quiet, and simply exhale and inhale.

Don't pressure yourself by saying, "I *must* spend an hour a day centering my life or having a devotion time." Some women, especially those with young children scrambling in nonstop motion, can find it difficult to carve out ten minutes to be alone—and that tends to come at their own bath time. Her *breathe* time might be the five minutes she is rocking her baby to sleep! A longer *breathe* and *believe* time once a week may be more realistic for her.

For years, I carved out a time to read my Bible by showing up a few minutes early outside my child's school in the afternoon. I miss those times! They were quiet moments when I could sit in my car alone, praise music playing softly on the radio, and my Bible in my lap propped up on the steering wheel.

Never feel guilty for taking a few minutes to talk to the Lord or quietly reflect on your relationship with Him or read a passage of Scripture. These moments have an eternal quality to them that can make them the *most* beneficial moments in a day. Others may see you as "escaping" reality, but in truth you are embracing the ultimate reality. Some may regard you as "loafing," but in truth you are engaged in a spiritual discipline that is intentional and productive.

Sometimes the best times for an affirmation of what you believe are the moments between your awakening in the morning and your getting out of bed. For me, that is a prime time to say, "I am loved by You, God. I know that You have a plan and purpose for my day. I give this day to You. Lead me into all that You have for me to give, to receive, and to experience."

One of my beloved verses for believing is:

You are my hiding place;
you will protect me from trouble
and surround me with songs of deliverance. (Psalm 32:7)

I encourage you to pause and reflect on the many ways the Lord is your hiding place in today's troubled world.

Feeling Ready to Bounce Back

How can you tell when you are *ready* to bounce back?

For me, there is a moment when I feel ready for whatever comes next. I have a sense of peace, and at the same time a sense of enthusiasm and energy.

I'm most ready to bounce back when I am fully assured of God's forgiveness and have laid down at His feet all of my sins, failures, worries, fears, and other negative emotions. I no longer have spiritual entanglements or emotional burdens. I feel *free* to bounce back!

I'm ready to bounce back when I feel ready to "fight" again. My fight is twofold. It is against the devil. But it also is *for* something. Very often a person is wiser to fight *for* their loved ones rather than to see themselves in a battle against Satan. A woman will often move heaven and earth, if possible, to help her children or spouse. Fighting *for* the things of the Lord is a valiant fight and one the Lord promises to help us win.

I'm also ready to bounce back when I feel ready—even enthusiastically eager—to take a risk in trusting God for something I know is pleasing to Him and is according to His will.

You may think you've done everything you can do . . . and you may have. But is it possible that you've started to think God has done everything *He* can do? The truth is He hasn't! There's still *more* that God can do. Always.

Today may very well be the exciting day when you take a new risk with your faith.

Trust God to do something more . . . bigger . . . better.

And . . . then . . .

Bounce back!

Reflection Guide

The following Bible verses, comments, applications, and questions are intended for your ongoing reflection and application. You may choose to do this alone or with a group—or perhaps both alone and with a group.

I encourage you to recognize at the outset that there is a distinct difference between reflection and application, and to do both.

Reflection

Reflection is thinking about something. It is contemplating, meditating upon, or considering. There is much to be gained by weighing information—seeing multiple facets of meaning and seeking to gain understanding. The opinions of others can help you in this process, but make sure that the number-one source of all opinions in your personal or group study is God's opinion, which is readily available in God's Word.

If you don't have a study Bible, you will benefit from finding one that you like and understand. There are many good study Bibles available, in various versions and translations, and with different types and amounts of additional information to help you understand what the Scriptures teach.

Application

Application moves information from the realms of knowledge and understanding into the realm of behavior. As you read, discuss, and reflect on the lessons that follow, set your mind to asking continually, "How can I put this into *action* in my life? How can I use this? Do this? Live this out in my daily routine?"

God doesn't give us His Word to make us smart. He gives us His Word so we can embody it on this earth and, in so doing, reap rewards that are eternal and blessings that are for extending His plans and purposes on this earth.

As you read and study, ask yourself questions such as these:

- What would I be wise to change in my life? What would I be wise to add or to eliminate?
- What are the practical steps that the Lord seems to be prompting me to take?
- Who might be willing to help me implement changes in my life—in a healthy, mutually dependent way?
- What must I do solely with God's help?
- Is there a sequence to how God wants me to make changes in the near future?
- What is the best and highest application I can make of these insights into God's Word to expand God's plans and purposes on the earth?

Keep a Journal

I strongly encourage you to purchase a small journal to write down your personal reflections and statements of application. Choose your own style and size of journal. You may want to incorporate what you write into a personal journal that you are already using—but do give these topics their own space within that journal.

Pray about What You Write

I suggest you pray before you undertake each topic of study, and then pray again as you complete your study and your note making. Ask the Lord at the outset of your study to give you His peace, an ability to focus on what you are reading and thinking, and insights into His Word. Ask Him to speak to your innermost spirit about His highest desires for you.

Thank God for His Help

Then, as you complete your time of study, thank Him for His presence with you always. Thank Him for the guidance, direction, comfort, and challenge you have experienced. And ask Him to seal in your heart and mind the truth of His Word and to help you as you seek to act on His directives.

Guidelines for Group Study

Every group needs a facilitator. This person must be willing to let each person in the group express herself fully, but not allow any one person to dominate a study session. The facilitator should also be free to offer her insights, without lecturing or "preaching" her opinions. The facilitator should seek to involve every person in a discussion by intentionally *asking* from time to time questions such as these: "What do *you* see in this verse? What do *you* find challenging in this question? How do *you* respond to this quote?" Ask for, but do not force, an answer or insist on participation. Some of those in your group may need a few weeks to feel confident or comfortable before sharing from their heart.

Recognize that not everybody in your group has your same background, your degree of understanding about various Bible teachings, or your same goals and purpose in life. Allow for these variations. Your role is not to teach others or correct others, but to *encourage* others to seek God's guidance in their life and to do what God leads them to do.

Group study of God's Word and books such as *Bounce Back!* can be very encouraging and uplifting to a woman in pain. There can be great comfort in spending time with women who have faced or are facing difficult times and who are seeking the help of the Lord in persevering through tough circumstances. A time of group discussion can produce tremendous emotional healing and strength.

Ask the Lord how He may desire for you to interact with others—and then experience the joy and comfort of sharing!

Introduction—Face the Trouble Behind the Smile

Our Part and God's Part

The psalmist perhaps knew a wider spectrum of pain and troubles than any other person in Bible times—over more years and in more circumstances. The Psalms are an expression of just about every emotion a person can experience.

As you begin your study of this book, examine closely two of my favorite psalms, Psalm 30 and Psalm 46. Go through them line by line and, as you do, consider these questions:

What does God call us to do?

What does God tell us He will do on our behalf?

What are we to say when we feel ourselves in emotional pain?

How does God see our time of difficulty? And how does that differ from the way we tend to see our own difficulty and pain?

I will exalt you, LORD,
> for you lifted me out of the depths
> and did not let my enemies gloat over me.
LORD my God, I called to you for help,
> and you healed me.
You, LORD, brought me up from the realm of
> the dead;
> you spared me from going down into the pit.

Sing the praises of the LORD, you his
> faithful people;
> praise his holy name.
For his anger lasts only a moment,
> but his favor lasts a lifetime;
weeping may stay for the night,
> but rejoicing comes in the morning.

When I felt secure, I said,
> "I will never be shaken."

Lord, when you favored me,
    you made my royal mountain stand firm;
but when you hid your face,
    I was dismayed.

To you, Lord, I called;
    to the Lord I cried for mercy:
"What is gained if I am silenced,
    if I go down to the pit?
Will the dust praise you?
    Will it proclaim your faithfulness?
Hear, Lord, and be merciful to me;
    Lord, be my help."

You turned my wailing into dancing;
    you removed my sackcloth and clothed me
    with joy,
that my heart may sing your praises and not be silent.
    Lord my God, I will praise you forever. (Psalm 30)

God is our refuge and strength,
    an ever-present help in trouble.
Therefore we will not fear, though the earth
    give way
    and the mountains fall into the heart of the sea,
though its waters roar and foam
    and the mountains quake with their surging.

There is a river whose streams make glad the city
of God,
the holy place where the Most High dwells.
God is within her, she will not fall;
God will help her at break of day.
Nations are in uproar, kingdoms fall;
he lifts his voice, the earth melts.

The LORD Almighty is with us,
the God of Jacob is our fortress.
Come and see what the LORD has done,
the desolations he has brought on the earth.
He makes wars cease
to the ends of the earth.
He breaks the bow and shatters the spear;
he burns the shields with fire.
He says, "Be still, and know that I am God;
I will be exalted among the nations,
I will be exalted in the earth."
The LORD Almighty is with us;
the God of Jacob is our fortress. (Psalm 46)

Being Still, Knowing God

Consider the questions below as they relate to God's command
in Psalm 46:10: "Be still, and know that I am God."

- What does it mean for a person to become still?
- How difficult is it for us to become still—especially in our world today, and especially when we are almost frantic with inner pain and struggle?
- What are practical ways in which we can become still?
- Why must we become still before the Lord?
- What does it mean to "know that God is God"?

Chapter 1—Decide to Breathe, Believe, and Bounce Back

Making Decisions

If making a decision is an "activation of the human will," how important is it that we learn to make decisions and have the courage not only to make decisions, but follow through on them?

Do you make decisions with timidity or boldness? Are you confident in the decisions you make? Why or why not?

Do you feel empowered to make decisions regarding your own schedule, likes and dislikes, and your own set of beliefs and values? Why or why not?

Breathing

Have you ever been so hurt that you just wanted to run away and hide? What did you do? What happened? Reflect on that experience.

Are there specific things that you know you need to "put off" before you can "put on" something better?

Is it important to you to separate yourself from current surroundings periodically in order to experience the presence of the Lord in a new and refreshing way? In what ways can a woman separate herself in a given day without leaving her home or leaving town?

Where do *you* go to take time for personal reflection and evaluation of your own life, goals, and activities?

Believing

If someone asked you to describe in just a few sentences what you believe about God, what would you say? (Suggestion: write down your statement.)

What are the top seven values you hold as unalterable? List them.

Set aside your statements of belief and values for a few days. Then revisit them. Are there changes you want to make? (You can repeat this process as many times as you like. Keep refining your statements to reflect your true core beliefs and values.)

Revisiting Notable Statements of Belief

Below are two of the foremost creeds that were developed in the first few centuries after the life, death, and resurrection of Jesus. These creeds have been recited by Christians of all nations, races, and cultures for nearly two thousand years.

Do you find yourself gravitating to one of these creeds more than to the other? Why?

The Apostles' Creed

I believe in God the Father Almighty, maker of
heaven and earth;
And in Jesus Christ His only Son our Lord:
who was conceived by the Holy Spirit, born of
the Virgin Mary, suffered under Pontius Pilate,
was crucified, dead, and buried; He descended
into hades; the third day He rose from the
dead; He ascended into heaven, and sitteth at
the right hand of God the Father Almighty;
from thence He shall come to judge the quick
and the dead.
I believe in the Holy Spirit, the holy Christian
church, the communion of saints, the
forgiveness of sins, the resurrection of the
body, and the life everlasting. Amen.

The Nicene Creed

I believe in one God, the Father Almighty, Maker
of heaven and earth, and of all things visible
and invisible.
And in one Lord Jesus Christ, the only-begotten
Son of God, begotten of the Father before all
worlds; God of God, Light of Light, very God
of very God; begotten, not made, being of one
substance with the Father, by whom all things
were made.

Who, for us men for our salvation, came down
    from heaven,
    and was incarnate by the Holy Spirit of the
    Virgin Mary,
    and was made man; and was crucified also for
    us under Pontius Pilate;
He suffered and was buried, and the third day
    He rose again,
    according to the Scriptures, and ascended
    into heaven,
    and sits on the right hand of the Father;
and He shall come again, with glory, to judge the
    quick and the dead;
    whose kingdom shall have no end.
And I believe in the Holy Spirit, the Lord and
    Giver of Life, who proceeds from the Father
    [and the Son]; who with the Father and the
    Son together is worshiped and glorified; who
    spoke by the prophets.
And I believe in one catholic and apostolic Church.
    I acknowledge one baptism for the remission
    of sins; and I look for the resurrection of the
    dead, and the life of the world to come. Amen.

Writing Your Personal Statement of Belief

Now write out a statement of your most basic beliefs about God.
Try to limit your statement to fewer than three hundred words.

Give yourself some time with this. Read the creeds above for ideas of concepts to include in your own statement of beliefs. Allow yourself the opportunity to read and reread what you write, and to edit your statement as you feel God speaking to your heart.

Write your own personal statement of belief in your journal.

Inspiring Yourself with the Word of God

Do you have a favorite set of verses—ones that have been used by the Lord to inspire you, convict you, or give direction to your life? List them. Review them. (Suggestion: write them down, perhaps on 3x5-inch note cards.)

Bouncing Back

Do you believe it is possible for a person to bounce back from all painful circumstances or situations?

Why is it important to bounce back?

What does it mean to you to move onward?

What does it mean to you to move forward?

What does it mean to you to move upward?

Give personal examples that illustrate your answers.

Chapter 2—Reclaim Your Lost Time and Opportunity

Nothing Is Wasted

Do you feel that you have wasted time in a relationship . . . a job . . . or the pursuit of a specific goal or endeavor? If so, why?

Reflect on the concept that a Christian truly can never

"waste" time because the Lord is always eager to redeem what we do for our good and for the good of His purposes on the earth. What must we do to put our time into the category of "redeemable" by the Lord?

How are time, opportunities, and our personal priorities interrelated?

Death and Disease

Has someone or something died—leaving behind a gaping hole of emptiness and grief? Or has an accident or illness left you or a loved one with diminished physical capacity?

Ask the Lord to heal your sorrow. Ask Him to direct you to godly people who can love you and comfort you as if they are embracing you with the everlasting arms of the Lord.

If you have experienced grief in the past, what was the single most helpful thing that you did or that someone said to you or did for you?

Failure

Have you experienced a time of failure? Have you given in to a temptation and fallen into a web of sin and its consequences? Ask the Lord to forgive you and free you.

If you have faced and overcome a failure in the past, what did you do to pick yourself up, dust yourself off, and move on?

Disappointment

Is it time to let go of a dream that you have held for a long time? Ask the Lord to give you a new dream—*His* dream for your future.

Is there something that you once dreamed but no longer dream for your life? Was the old dream one of your design? If the dream was of the Lord, is there a vestige of that dream lingering? If so, ask the Lord to show you how to recapture that dream, with alterations that make it truly His dream for you today.

Rejection

Are you struggling with rejection? If so, write a statement about the way you feel. Step back from that statement for a day or two and then revisit what you have written. Do you feel that you deserved to be rejected? If so, why? What do you believe the Lord says to any of His beloved children who feel rejected?

Has your self-identity or self-value taken a hit? What might you do to regain a sense of your own identity, authenticity, or value? (Hint: start by asking the Lord to restore your soul!)

Read the Song of Solomon in the Old Testament. Read it aloud softly and slowly to yourself. As you read, keep in mind that this is God's love song to His people. And you are His beloved child today! Take this song as one that the Lord Jesus is personally singing to you.

Experiencing the Pasture of the Good Shepherd

Read and reflect on these familiar verses below. Pause after each line to ask yourself, "What does the Lord want me to hear Him saying in my spirit?"

The LORD is my shepherd; I shall not want.

He makes me lie down in green pastures.

He leads me beside still waters.

> He restores my soul.

He leads me in paths of righteousness

> for his name's sake.

Even though I walk through the valley of the

> shadow of death,

> I will fear no evil,

for you are with me;

> your rod and your staff,

> they comfort me.

You prepare a table before me

> in the presence of my enemies;

you anoint my head with oil;

> my cup overflows.

Surely goodness and mercy shall follow me

> all the days of my life,

and I shall dwell in the house of the LORD forever.

> (Psalm 23 ESV)

Now go back and make each line of this psalm a personal prayer. For example: "O Lord, I am trusting You today to be my shepherd. I am relying fully on You to meet all the needs of my life with such full provision that there isn't anything I lack. I am asking You to show me the difference between my needs and my wants. Please show me the green pastures that You have for meeting my needs. Help me to stay there and not wander off into pastures that may seem greener from my own limited human perspective. Lead me to the quiet waters where I can be refreshed in You . . . " (And so forth.)

As you read, contemplate, and pray, envision a beautiful natural setting and see with spiritual eyes the way in which the Lord might meet you in that place.

Giving All Time and Opportunity to God

In what ways might a woman give all time and opportunity to God? How does having this perspective of yielding time and tasks to God give a woman freedom from bitterness or sorrow?

Reflect on these verses:

We go through exactly what Christ goes through. If we go through the hard times with him, then we're certainly going to go through the good times with him! (Romans 8:17 MSG)

[The Spirit] knows us far better than we know ourselves, knows our pregnant condition, and keeps us present before God. That's why we can be so sure that every detail in our lives of love for God is worked into something good. (Romans 8:27–28 MSG)

Chapter 3—Overcome Your Exhaustion and Stress

Evaluating Your Stress Level

On a scale of one to ten (with one being no stress and ten being extreme stress), where do you put your stress level today? Is this an aberration, or is this the general stress level you have felt for some time? Do you want this level of stress to continue? If not, what are you going to do about it?

Managing Your Time

I often say to women, "If the devil can't make you bad, he'll make you busy." I find he often moves against us to wear us out so we will have no energy to love others in the name of the Lord. Are you busier now than ever before in your life? Is this a possible trick of the enemy?

What might you do to

- reorganize your own schedule?
- readjust your priorities?
- find new ways of doing things more efficiently or delegating chores to others?

Take a blank calendar—perhaps one organized by weeks— and write down those things that you consider to be "musts." Then, and only then, consider where you might fit in other things that you would "like" to do in a given week. Force yourself to leave at least ten blank hours in any week. (Yes, it is doable.)

Managing Your Obligations

Make a list of all the personal obligations that you have—to individuals, to groups, to organizations (including your church).

Pray about each of these responsibilities. Are these obligations ones that the Lord has asked you to take on? If so, you can trust Him to give you the ideas, energy, and resources to do what He has called you to do. If not, ask Him to reveal to you which of your current obligations are ones that He wants you to continue.

Ask God if there is another obligation or responsibility that He would like for you to undertake in place of a current obligation or responsibility.

Managing Your Drive to Succeed

Is there anything in your life that you have been striving to do for some time (perhaps weeks, months, or years) without any significant degree of success?

Is this the time to let that go? Or is it time to regroup, change course, move in another direction?

Ask the Lord to help you make wise decisions.

Anticipating the Peace of Christ

Jesus said, "I have told you these things, so that in me you may have peace. In this world you will have trouble. But take heart! I have overcome the world" (John 16:33).

Jesus made it clear that our peace is to be found in *Him*, not in our circumstances or the world around us. Do you have a personal example in your life that leads you to respond to this verse, "Yes, I know that to be true!"?

In what ways do you find spiritual immunity from the troubles of this world?

Planning Your Personal Retreat

If you are feeling overly committed or stressed out, schedule at least four days away for a personal, private retreat. Plan to get away to a place where you truly can experience beauty and rest in a safe, private location. (You might even consider sending your family or roommates away and making your own home the place for your "retreat"—unplugging your phone and all electronic devices.)

With your notebook and Bible in hand, ask the Lord to show you what He desires for you. Ask Him to impart to you peace, purpose, and a sense of delight at His presence.

Ask God to show you how much He loves you and how He longs to see you *enjoy* your life and the relationships He has sent your way.

Begin to breathe. Reaffirm what you believe. Ask the Lord to show you specifics ways to bounce back into your daily life.

Verses for Reflection

As you set aside time to breathe and reaffirm what you believe, take time to meditate on the passages of Scripture below.

- Circle words that stand out to you as you read these passages line by line.
- What new insights do you have into these verses?
- How might you apply the principles in these words of wisdom?

He gives strength to the weary
    and increases the power of the weak.
Even youths grow tired and weary,
    and young men stumble and fall;
but those who hope in the LORD
    will renew their strength.

> They will soar on wings like eagles;
>> they will run and not grow weary,
>> they will walk and not be faint. (Isaiah
>> 40:29–31)

> In peace I will lie down and sleep,
>> for you alone, LORD,
>> make me dwell in safety. (Psalm 4:8)

> "Be still, and know that I am God;
>> I will be exalted among the nations,
>> I will be exalted in the earth."
> The LORD Almighty is with us;
>> the God of Jacob is our fortress.
>> (Psalm 46:10–11)

Chapter 4—Break Out of Your Limitations

Springing the Traps, Loosing the Bonds

Is there something that is constraining you from the pursuit of your God-given dreams and goals? Do you feel trapped in any way?

Are you constrained by circumstances? If so, what are they? (Be specific.) What might you do to break free?

Are you constrained by someone who is holding you back or keeping you down? If so, are they functioning in a careless way, a purposeful way, or an abusive way? What might you do to remove yourself from this person's influence or abusive behavior?

Are you constrained by your own thoughts and feelings? (For example, have you developed a compulsive or obsessive way of thinking? Are you caught in a cycle of unforgiveness? Do you have abiding feelings of vengeance, jealousy, anger, or bitterness?)

How are your own thoughts and feelings holding you back or suppressing your energy or creativity? What might you do to end the cycle of thoughts and feelings that are *not* beneficial?

Taking a Step Toward Freedom

On the next page is a list of twenty circumstances or situations that people often feel are constraining or limiting. Next to each one, indicate in the first column, labeled *Me*, if you have personally struggled with this in the past, or are presently struggling with it.

Are you not personally struggling with this issue or condition but know someone who seems to be struggling with it? If so, write that person's name in the second column, labeled *Another*.

Then, in the third column, *First Step*, write down one first step a person might take to greater freedom or perhaps the first step you took to experience greater freedom in this area of your life.

Finally, in the fourth column, labeled *God's Truth*, write a statement for each of these situations or conditions that you believe sums up how God feels about a person who is trapped in this circumstance or situation.

	Me	Another	First Step	God's Truth
1. Racial prejudice				
2. Poverty or extreme debt				
3. Abusive relationship				
4. Physical ailment (long-standing or permanent)				
5. Dead-end job				
6. Social ostracism				
7. Injustice, victim of crime				
8. Personal fears				
9. Obsessive, compulsive, or limiting cycles of negative thoughts and feelings				
10. Recurring depression				
11. Language barriers or communication difficulties				
12. Guilt over past sins				
13. Shame related to behavior of others				
14. Natural disaster, war, or tragedy that resulted in extreme loss				
15. Age (discrimination)				
16. Persecution related to beliefs or faith				
17. Lack of information, education, or skills				
18. Obligations to family members (excessive)				
19. Imprisonment (actual prison) or confinement as a hostage				
20. Limitations related to cultural or religious domination				

Are there other specific ties that bind you or someone you love? Identify and evaluate them.

Trusting God

Trust begins with our believing that God desires to help us when we are experiencing any injustice, sickness, debt, or abandonment, or when the walls seem to be pressing in on all sides. God's Word says:

> Since then we have a great high priest who has passed through the heavens, Jesus, the Son of God, let us hold fast our confession. For we do not have a high priest who is unable to sympathize with our weaknesses, but one who in every respect has been tempted as we are, yet without sin. Let us then with confidence draw near to the throne of grace, that we may receive mercy and find grace to help in time of need. (Hebrews 4:14–16 ESV)

What insights do you have into these verses? Do you believe its message for *your* circumstances?

Verses of Encouragement

Below are four passages of Scripture that speak of God's desire and ability to help a person bounce back or break free of limiting, confining circumstances. Next to each verse, write a statement about how you personally believe God has helped you, or might help you based upon the truth of His Word.

After you have suffered a little while, the God of all grace . . . will himself restore, confirm, strengthen, and establish you. (1 Peter 5:10 ESV)

What definitions do you give to the words below?

Restore:

Confirm:

Strengthen:

Establish:

He who began a good work in you will carry it on to completion until the day of Christ Jesus. (Philippians 1:6)

Fixing our eyes on Jesus, the pioneer and perfecter of faith. (Hebrews 12:2)

What strategies can a person use to keep her eyes fixed on Jesus?

Define these terms in your own words:
Author:

Perfecter:

"For my thoughts are not your thoughts,
 neither are your ways my ways,"
  declares the LORD.

"As the heavens are higher than the earth,

so are my ways higher than your ways

and my thoughts than your thoughts.

As the rain and the snow

come down from heaven,

and do not return to it

without watering the earth

and making it bud and flourish,

so that it yields seed for the sower

and bread for the eater,

so is my word that goes out from my mouth:

It will not return to me empty,

but will accomplish what I desire

and achieve the purpose for which I sent it.

You will go out in joy

and be led forth in peace;

the mountains and hills

will burst into song before you,

and all the trees of the field

will clap their hands.

Instead of the thornbush will grow the juniper,

and instead of briers the myrtle will grow.

This will be for the LORD's renown,

for an everlasting sign,

that will endure forever."

(Isaiah 55:8–13)

Chapter 5—Say No to Despair

Anticipating the Lord's Favor

Set aside an hour to contemplate deeply one of the most encouraging chapters in the Bible: Isaiah 61.

Keep in mind that Jesus promised He would send the Spirit of the Lord to every person who believes in Jesus as the Son of God. As a Christian, your life is a reflection of Christ's life. You are not the Savior of the world, but you *are* called by God to reflect His character and to say and do what He said and did. This chapter shows how God sees you and your role on this earth.

As you read and meditate on this chapter, ask yourself repeatedly:

- How might the Lord *do* this in my life?
- How can I bring greater honor and glory to the Lord?
- In what ways might I grow in my ability to "delight greatly in the Lord"?

The Spirit of the Sovereign LORD is on me,
> because the LORD has anointed me
> to proclaim good news to the poor.
He has sent me to bind up the brokenhearted,
> to proclaim freedom for the captives
> and release from darkness for the prisoners,
to proclaim the year of the LORD's favor
> and the day of vengeance of our God,

to comfort all who mourn,
    and provide for those who grieve in Zion—
to bestow on them a crown of beauty
    instead of ashes,
the oil of joy
    instead of mourning,
and a garment of praise
    instead of a spirit of despair.
They will be called oaks of righteousness,
    a planting of the LORD
    for the display of his splendor.

They will rebuild the ancient ruins
    and restore the places long devastated;
they will renew the ruined cities
    that have been devastated for generations.
Strangers will shepherd your flocks;
    foreigners will work your fields and vineyards.
And you will be called priests of the LORD,
    you will be named ministers of our God.
You will feed on the wealth of nations,
    and in their riches you will boast.

Instead of your shame
    you will receive a double portion,
and instead of disgrace
    you will rejoice in your inheritance.
And so you will inherit a double portion in
    your land,
    and everlasting joy will be yours.

"For I, the LORD, love justice;

    I hate robbery and wrongdoing.

In my faithfulness I will reward my people

    and make an everlasting covenant with them.

Their descendants will be known among

    the nations

    and their offspring among the peoples.

All who see them will acknowledge

    that they are a people the LORD has blessed."

I delight greatly in the LORD;

    my soul rejoices in my God.

For he has clothed me with garments of salvation

    and arrayed me in a robe of his righteousness,

as a bridegroom adorns his head like a priest,

    and as a bride adorns herself with her jewels.

For as the soil makes the sprout come up

    and a garden causes seeds to grow,

so the Sovereign LORD will make righteousness

    and praise spring up before all nations.

    (Isaiah 61)

Confronting the Devil's Tactics of Fear and Lies

Have you ever had an experience in your life in which you felt thoroughly confused, incapable of discerning God's will from the devil's lies? What happened?

How did you discern right from wrong, or the tactics of evil that were coming against you? How did you fight back?

Have you ever had an experience in which you found yourself in a panic—or an extreme bout or period of deep fear? What happened?

Have you ever had a deep and abiding fear that you just couldn't seem to shake? What did you do?

Of all the things in the world that a person might find frightening, what scares *you* the most?

As Elijah did, have you ever heard God speaking to you in a still, small voice in the depths of your soul? Write or share a few words about that experience and what it meant to you at the time . . . and what it means to you now.

Overcoming Fears with Faith

The apostle Paul wrote to his colleague and protégé Timothy, "For the Spirit God gave us does not make us timid, but gives us power, love and self-discipline" (2 Timothy 1:7).

How does this verse challenge your faith?

In what ways might you feel a need to believe God can give you *more* spiritual power, love, and self-discipline?

Dispelling the Darkness

The Word of God—both Jesus the Word and the written Word we call the Bible—is described as light giving. Through the centuries, Bible commentators have used the phrase "a stream of light" to describe words of faith spoken from the mouth of a Christian. Can you picture this?

What importance does the concept of giving light place upon the words a person speaks during times of fear or depression?

Consider these two statements about light:

"I am the light of the world. Whoever follows me will never walk in darkness, but will have the light of life" (John 8:12).

> In what ways does Jesus give you light?
> How are light and life related?

Your word is a lamp to my feet and a light to my path. (Psalm 119:105 ESV)

> Can you recall a time when hearing or speaking the Word of God helped to brighten a time of fear or depression?
> Were there specific words or Scriptures that seemed especially effective in building your faith?

Identifying Helpful Others

It is especially important in bouncing back from depression that a person be willing to re-integrate others into their life—especially those who have proven themselves to be beneficial!

Identify today one or more people you can trust to

- be a source of encouragement;
- be there when you need a shoulder to lean on;
- speak the truth of God to you;
- share a good laugh with you.

What might you do to rekindle or cultivate your relationship with each of these people?

Chapter 6—Cure Your
Loneliness by Adding Love

Are You Lonely?

Have you ever struggled with strong feelings of isolation or loneliness? Have you ever felt alone in a crowd? What did you do?

Recall the best advice you have ever heard about how to survive loneliness in a relationship that should be loving but isn't.

Reflect on the following passage from the Psalms:

> Sing to God, sing in praise of his name,
>> extol him who rides on the clouds;
>> rejoice before him—his name is the LORD.
> A father to the fatherless, a defender of widows,
>> is God in his holy dwelling.
> God sets the lonely in families,
>> he leads out the prisoners with singing.
>> (Psalm 68:4–6)

How might voicing praise to the Lord help a person overcome feelings of loneliness?

To the Jews, orphans and widows held a special place because they were perceived to be the most vulnerable and needy people in their society. They were truly "alone" in life. The Jews were commanded by God to take care of the widows and orphans, but God alone was revered as their source of ultimate protection and provision. Today, women who are widowed or divorced—

and children who have lost parents to death or who have experienced divorce—are often the loneliest people in our society.

What responsibility do we in the church have for our widows and orphans?

In what ways have you experienced the Lord's presence as your greatest comfort when you have been alone or isolated?

Jesus' Commands to Love

Reflect on the following verses about God's command for us to love others:

> This is my commandment, that you love one another as I have loved you. (John 15:12 ESV)

> As the Father has loved me, so have I loved you. Now remain in my love. If you keep my commands, you will remain in my love, just as I have kept my Father's commands and remain in his love. (John 15:9–10)

Identify several practical ways that you can manifest love as Jesus commanded His disciples at the time of the Last Supper.

The Freeing Power of Forgiveness

Have you ever felt isolated from others because of things they have done or said that you feel incapable of forgiving? What did you do?

Respond to these words of Jesus:

> If you forgive other people when they sin against you, your heavenly Father will also forgive you. But if you do

not forgive others their sins, your Father will not forgive your sins. (Matthew 6:14–15)

Give, and it will be given to you. A good measure, pressed down, shaken together and running over, will be poured into your lap. For with the measure you use, it will be measured to you. (Luke 6:38)

Luke 6:38 is sometimes quoted to encourage people to believe for God's material or financial blessing. But what does it mean for you to read it as an admonition about the way we are to love and forgive others? Keep in mind that the verse immediately preceding this one says, "Forgive, and you will be forgiven" (Luke 6:37).

To whom might the Lord be sending you with opportunities to give love and to receive love?

What precautions does a person need to take in reaching out to others with love?

Chapter 7—A Stronger You

Directing Your "Bounce"

Consider what might be the differences between bouncing back and bouncing forward. Does every crisis in a person's life present an opportunity to do both?

Write a brief description of the way you see each process:

Bouncing back:

Bouncing forward:

Taking Inventory

Have you ever experienced a severe loss? Are you experiencing one now?

Write down *specific* things you feel you have lost. Consider some of the concepts below as being part of a loss:

Self-worth	Friends	Family loyalty
Provision	Protection	Positive attitude
Home	Finances/Money	Children
Self-confidence	Joy	Security
Peace of mind	Sleep	Health
Energy	Enthusiasm for life	Ability to have fun

Which of these are most important for you to regain, reestablish, or renew?

Scheduling Your Personal Retreat

Write out a description for an "Ideal Personal Retreat" that you would like to take within the next three months. Include where you would like to go, what you would do once there, what you would take with you to read (besides your Bible), and what you would hope to experience on this retreat.

Describe specific activities you might do on your personal retreat as part of

Breathing:

Believing:

Now set a date and go!

About the Author

Julie Clinton, M.Ad., MBA, president of Extraordinary Women, has spoken to hundreds of thousands of women as host of EWomen conferences all across America, and is author of *Extraordinary Women: Discovering the Dream God Created for You*, the devotional *Living God's Dream for You*, *10 Things You Aren't Telling Him*, and *A Woman's Path to Emotional Freedom*. A woman of deep faith, she cares passionately about seeing women live out their dreams by finding their freedom in Christ. Julie and her husband of thirty-three years, Tim, live in Virginia with their son, Zach. Her daughter, Megan, recently married to Ben Allison, lives nearby, and they often spend weekends together as a family.

WORTHY
PUBLISHING

IF YOU ENJOYED THIS BOOK, WILL YOU CONSIDER SHARING THE MESSAGE WITH OTHERS?

- Mention the book in a Facebook post, Twitter update, Pinterest pin, or blog post.

- Recommend this book to those in your small group, book club, workplace, and classes.

- Head over to facebook.com/worthypublishing, "LIKE" the page, and post a comment as to what you enjoyed the most.

- Tweet "I recommend reading #BounceBack by Julie Clinton @ewomen // @worthypub"

- Pick up a copy for someone you know who would be challenged and encouraged by this message.

- Write a book review online.

You can subscribe to Worthy Publishing's newsletter at worthypublishing.com.

**WORTHY PUBLISHING
FACEBOOK PAGE**

**WORTHY PUBLISHING
WEBSITE**